CARRYING IT FORWARD

OTHER TITLES
BY JOHN BRADY MCDONALD

Childhood Thoughts and Water
Electricity Slides
The Glass Lodge
Kitotam: He Speaks to It

Carrying It Forward

ESSAYS FROM KISTAHPINÂNIHK

John Brady McDonald

WOLSAK
& WYNN

Published by Wolsak and Wynn Publishers
280 James Street North
Hamilton, ON L8R2L3
www.wolsakandwynn.ca

Editor: Noelle Allen | Copy editor: Ashley Hisson
Cover and interior design: Marijke Friesen
Cover image: *Piskihtisiw* (*It Is Separated into Pieces*) by John Brady
    McDonald
Author photograph: Kymber Rae Photography
Typeset in Minion Pro
Printed by Brant Service Press Ltd., Brantford, Canada

Printed on certified 100% post-consumer Rolland Enviro Paper.

10 9 8 7 6 5 4 3 2 1

Canada Council   Conseil des arts
for the Arts   du Canada

ONTARIO ARTS COUNCIL
CONSEIL DES ARTS DE L'ONTARIO
an Ontario government agency
un organisme du gouvernement de l'Ontario

Canadä

The publisher gratefully acknowledges the support of the Ontario Arts Council, the Canada Council for the Arts and the Government of Canada.

Library and Archives Canada Cataloguing in Publication

Title: Carrying it forward : essays from Kistahpinânihk / John Brady
    McDonald.
Names: McDonald, John, 1981- author.
Identifiers: Canadiana 20220399972 | ISBN 9781989496596 (softcover)
Subjects: LCGFT: Essays.
Classification: LCC PS8625.D646 C37 2022 | DDC C814/.6—dc23

To my family, both here in the flesh
and those now Ancestors

Contents

By Way of Introduction

"Have you ever considered writing nonfiction?"

This was the question posed to me by Noelle Allen, publisher of Wolsak and Wynn, as she wrote to let me know that one of my manuscript submissions was not going to be published by them. It was the initial and very welcome invitation to the book that you are currently holding in your hands. Indeed, I had written nonfiction pieces many times, but having spent the better part of the last twenty years focused on literary fiction, performance art monologues and poetry, it had been quite a while since I had sat down and focused on committing nonfiction to paper.

Well, that's not *exactly* true – not if you count Facebook posts.

Since I joined social media back in 2011, there have been many times where I have gone off on long, expansive posts on various subjects, either of a serious nature or a more reflective, introspective one, usually sparked by current events or

1

the world around me. These weren't rants, by any stretch of the imagination. These were more like truncated editorial pieces sharing my opinions and thoughts about current topics, along with reminiscences of my childhood and nostalgic reminders of my glory days.

These social media posts filled a painful void for me. When my first book of poetry, *The Glass Lodge*, was published by Kegedonce Press in 2004, I was a young man, trying my best to express the life I was living – a life of addiction, gangs, racism and surviving the streets. That book soon had me touring Canada, presenting at the Ottawa International Writers Festival, the Ânskohk Aboriginal Literature Festival (where I shared the stage and a book-signing table with a soon-to-be-infamous Joseph Boyden) and the Eden Mills Writers' Festival, where I shared the stage with Drew Hayden Taylor, the late Lee Maracle and, in an interesting twist, Margaret Atwood, who stopped me afterwards to tell me that she enjoyed my reading. The photograph of me and Margaret Atwood after the reading is priceless. She's in a cute green floppy sun hat and green coat and shirt looking the epitome of the cultured Canadian writer – and then there's me, in an old army surplus jacket and a T-shirt from a tattoo parlour in Ottawa, with my goatee dyed blood red and a pentagram around my neck. I was flying here and there, doing book signings and press interviews, and being touted as some kind of wunderkind, a brash Indigenous writer from the Prairies with bold, frank things to say.

I assumed that with the success I thought I had achieved with my first collection, I was on my way to bigger and better

John Brady
McDonald and
Margaret Atwood,
Eden Mills Writers'
Festival, 2006.
Author's photo.

things. I was wrong – young, naive and wrong. It was an enjoyable but short-lived moment in the sun and at the point that picture was taken my time in the sun had pretty much run its course. I was on the road to nearly twenty years of rejection, obscurity and almost absolute literary and artistic reclusion.

Social media posts provided me with the ability to keep my name out there, even if it was simply a "yoo-hoo, remember me?" post lamenting my lost dream. For years, these posts were my only way of getting my words to the public. By the end of the decade, I had amassed around two hundred rejection letters, unsuccessfully attempted to crowdsource the funds to self-publish my works and given poetry readings to small crowds and, many times, to empty chairs.

The social media posts, however, gave me not only a way to vent, but also an instant gauge of what was going on in the Indigenous literary scene. They were a pressure release for someone who wanted his words seen and heard. They provided instant gratification, and the amount of "likes" that

3

your posts generated kept you going further and further. It became a desire, then almost an addiction.

I cannot pinpoint exactly when the mood of social media changed and became polarized and political. Perhaps it was the re-elections of Canadian Conservative prime minister Stephen Harper and United States president George W. Bush. Perhaps it was the time of Idle No More, or the re-emergence of white supremacy and the rise of the keyboard warrior, those trolls hiding behind the anonymity of the internet to spew vitriol and racism from the safety of the shadows. At some point, those of us who had been fighting racism, injustice, poverty, xenophobia and both upper and lower case C conservatism offline began to speak up and speak out against the garbage and negativity being posted online.

I have always felt that it is my responsibility, as someone who has a bit of ability to put my words and thoughts into cohesive sentences, to speak up and be an advocate for those who felt that they had no voice, or, when it came to situations like Missing and Murdered Indigenous Women, were no longer here to speak for themselves. That was my role as a warrior – to defend those who were unable to defend themselves.

As the online war of words escalated, so did the length of the comments we left on posts and in comments sections.

As the written jousting grew and grew, a strange side effect began to take place, or at least it did with me. As we argued and fought with these bigots and rednecks and narrow-minded individuals, it became apparent that the majority of these trolls were often not very well educated or well read.

Where it began as simply, perhaps arrogantly, correcting their grammatical and spelling errors as a way to undermine their negative rhetoric, it soon became a conscious effort by those of us who are very articulate to weaponize our words in such a way that in these verbal jousts and sparring matches our opponents were overwhelmingly outclassed and outgunned by our use of large words and complete sentences.

The goal was that they would either stop commenting on a post altogether because they couldn't understand or keep up with what we were saying, or finally they'd resort to telling us to "fuck off." There was a wonderfully childish feeling of superiority in winning these battles, but it was in the end, hopefully, a way to limit the damage that the trolling individuals were causing, either by getting them hopelessly bogged down in a verbal rabbit hole such that people stopped following along, or stopping them from commenting completely.

While the ultimate goal was to stand up to these bullies, bigots and cowards, I fully admit that it was immensely pleasurable to reply to a racist or conspiratorial comment with a lengthy, blistering dissertation on a topic. There is very little in life where I knowingly take egotistical pride for my actions, but these were circumstances in which I did.

There was, indeed, another victory being won by those of us who were choosing to engage in these battles of words. The stereotype of the uneducated, illiterate, poorly spoken (to western standards) Indigenous person is never too far from the collective consciousness of Canadian society. It is one of the many racial prejudices that have followed us for generations, in spite of the gains made by some of the greatest Indigenous orators, writers and thinkers of the past hundred years, such as Chief Dan George, Maria Campbell and my own grandfather Jim Brady. We as Indigenous people have been prohibited from speaking and conversing in our own mother tongues at various points throughout Canadian history. We have been forced to learn the foreign English and French languages, and while we learned these new words, we have, thankfully and perhaps hopefully, for the most part been able to retain at least our accents, if not our complete language.

Those of us with accents, however, run into another issue as we repeatedly have our intelligence and the credibility and even the meaning of our words questioned. We are judged by the ability of anglophone ears to understand what we are saying and need to fight the stereotypes of what our accents have represented. For example, I have a friend who is a theoretical physicist. I have listened to this highly intelligent man explain extremely complex theories based on the work of Michael Faraday. However, because he is from Alabama and his accent is thick, he is often mocked, because, to quote someone who laughed at him, "it's hard to take someone seriously when they sound like Foghorn Leghorn." I know highly educated newcomers to Canada in the fields of medicine who face seething hatred because of their accents on the phone and are too often told, "Can I speak to someone who speaks English?" I always say that one of the reasons prime-time medical dramas are so inaccurate is that they rarely, if ever, depict the verbal racial abuse suffered by physicians, nurses, technicians and receptionists at the hands of anglicized patients because they can't understand what the individual is saying.

One of the subconscious means of survival in western society for those of us who speak with accents is something called "code-switching," which is changing one's accent or cadence of speech to a more anglicized pattern, either to mollify anglicized listeners or to simply be treated humanely. I have a fairly thick Cree–West Flat accent, which is naturally present in my regular speech patterns, but there are many times when I have changed my speech pattern for even simple things like ordering food or calling a cab, which often would not show up if the caller had an Indigenous accent. In my younger years, I was always called upon to make phone calls of this nature because I could "sound white." For many individuals, their accent could be the difference between life or death. I have heard of cases where Indigenous women have called for help during attacks but were ignored because it sounded like "two Indians fighting."

In the world of social media, however, the power of one's words is not hampered by the baggage that comes with those who cannot understand what you're saying because of your accent.

However, there is a downside. If you were not on the ball, and you were not careful with your own argument or comment, how you phrased it; if your own grammar or spelling was poor; if you used the wrong *there, their, they're*; if your facts were wrong, etc., your rebuttal would be shot to hell. You opened yourself up for the same kind of embarrassment and criticism that you dished out. It became a game, and you had to keep your game up to snuff if you wanted to play it. As a result, you found yourself going over each word and phrase in your comment with a fine-toothed comb, editing and refining it, looking for synonyms that would make an argument stronger or make you look smarter. You became a much better writer in the process.

Becoming fastidious and careful with what you said and how you said it had another positive aspect – it forced you to become humble. In Nêhiyawak Tipi Teachings, one of the first lessons you learn is *tapahtêyimisowin*, humility. This teaching is at the core of why we as Indigenous people are resilient in spite of the generations of obstacles placed before us.

While many see human beings as superior to other creatures, we are but one of nearly nine million species of life on Mother Earth, and though we have the ability to speak, think, rationalize and create with our hands and efforts, we are animals and we lack certain traits that give other animals advantages over us. This initial understanding that we are not better or worse than any other creature is one of the first steps of humility. While it is okay to be proud of what you accomplished, this does not mean that you are worth more than anyone else, nor does it mean that you are worth less. It means that the skills you possess and provide are to be for the greater good of the people, and not for you alone.

In my language, the word for *storytelling* is *âcimostakewin*, and the word for *storyteller* is *otâcimow*. These are somewhat sacred roles within Indigenous culture, for the storyteller is tasked with the responsibility of both passing along the knowledge and legends of the People, and doing so in a way that will entertain and engage. It can be a delicate act, particularly in the technological, "skip ad" world we live in today.

I have often considered writing either an autobiography or a memoir, but I have never been able to bring myself to do it, partly out of a feeling of pretentiousness, partly out of a fear that those who remember the events differently than me will attempt to gaslight me or call me a liar, but mostly out of fear of the monumental task it would be. Every attempt at an autobiography would result in the same thing: I would type the words, "I was born on a frigid February night in Prince Albert, Saskatchewan," then I would go no further.

This collection is not my autobiography, nor is it a collection of anecdotes from an individual who has had the opportunity to experience some amazing and life-changing things over the past forty years. These are the much-expanded thoughts, editorial commentary and philosophies that I have shared on my social media over the years, making myself vulnerable and open to criticism and the court of public opinion. These essays and editorial pieces are my way of sharing my opinions and thoughts in a more cohesive, direct manner, as opposed to my spoken word performances or my poetry.

In this collection I also go into detail about the events that led up to my July 2000 protest at the University of Cambridge, England, where I symbolically "discovered," then "claimed" England for the First Peoples of the Americas. For the first time ever, I have written down the story behind what happened that day, and the shock waves that it sent through my life and my career.

Also included in this collection is the essay "The Verdict," which was originally published in *Grain*. This piece, first published during the chaos and pain after the non-guilty verdict of the killer of Colten Boushie, marked one of the first times that I had returned to print in nearly a decade, though it is one of the pieces I wish that I had never been given the "inspiration" to write.

If there is a common theme going forward, you will see that I am constantly returning to and referencing my cultural identity, my heritage and my relatives. I am writing this fore-word as the Indigenous arts community is reeling from the revelation that the director and co-producer of the CBC television hit series *Trickster*, based on the amazing novel *Son of a Trickster* by Eden Robinson, has been knowingly claiming Indigenous ancestry, as well as employment positions and awards meant for Indigenous artists, without having tangible, acknowledged and solid connections to Indigenous heritage.

As a light-skinned Indigenous man who was originally named John A. McDonald at birth (during the writing of this book, through the help of the National Centre for Truth and Reconciliation, I legally changed my name to John Brady McDonald, leaving behind forty years of sharing the moni-ker of a man whose ambition of Manifest Destiny helped lead to the horrors of the residential school system I would one day find myself in), my struggle to be acknowledged as an Indigenous person was already difficult, and I have spent my adult life ensuring that I let people know that I am Indigenous. This recent tragedy in the Indigenous arts scene has reopened so many wounds within me that I have found myself returning to those ancestors, my grandparents and that family lineage and community identity and acceptance in order to heal. I acknowledge my privilege many times in this book, and I am grateful for the luck I have to be part of an amazing lineage. The ancient Egyptians had a philosophy that has always resonated with me. They said, "To speak the name of the dead is to make them live again." When I mention these individuals, I hope that I can provide an opportunity for their stories to be carried forward, and their memory to be brought to others and never forgotten.

In returning to that notion of *tapahtêyimisowin*, it is important to show humility by acknowledging the efforts of other individuals, and to never forget to acknowledge those who have helped along the way.

First and foremost, I would like to thank Noelle Allen and the team at Wolsak and Wynn for providing me with the opportunity to create this book. Noelle took the time to acknowledge what I had to say and has been wonderfully supportive in providing me with this platform with which to do so.

I wish to thank the members of my family, connected either by blood or by choice, who have accepted and supported what I have done and, more importantly, what I have to say, without judgment, ridicule or contempt. When one's life has often been unbelievable, it is an amazing feeling to be supported.

I wish to thank all of those people who, during my beginning years, took chance after chance upon me, believing that one day I would overcome the obstacles and trauma, and make something of myself. I hope that for every person who said, "Let's give him a chance," from the amazing teachers who kept fighting for me when I was a little asshole in the schools, to those who let me step up to the mic to sing or speak, to the amazing individuals who provided me with the opportunity to expand my world beyond the city blocks of my youth to across the country and eventually around the world, I have provided a suitable return on your investment, and I hope that, one day and every day, I have the opportunity to do the same for another young person, somewhere.

I wish to thank all of the complete strangers and occasional acquaintances who have supported me and my work over the past twenty years and who have never allowed me to give up on myself, my dreams or my work, those whose paths have crossed my own over the years and who shared those moments with me, be they ever so small in time, but deep in meaning.

I thank those who came before me and laid the groundwork that allowed those of us who followed them to go forward a little easier than they did. The Chinese have a saying, "Those who drink the water must remember those who dug the well." I thank you immensely for digging the well.

I remember reading the words of an Elder from Treaty Six Territory collected in 1976. He spoke of how, in the generations before, when an Elder was providing counsel and guidance, they would stick a knife into the ground before them and say, "If any of you are offended by what I have to say, then you can use this knife on me." That is the ultimate conviction in one's words, and when one makes such a bold statement, it shows that they truly believe in what they say.

In our culture, you do not go around referring to yourself as an Elder. That is a title bestowed upon you by the community, and to call yourself an Elder is seen as one of the highest forms of arrogance and haughtiness. If you are truly an Elder, then others will seek you out and call you one, not the other way around. I have never been referred to as an Elder, and I am sure that I would be uncomfortable being referred to as such. I have been called a Knowledge Keeper, which is someone who has been asked to provide cultural teachings and wisdom, and, for a while, I was somewhat comfortable with that label.

Recently, however, after my first cultural ceremony since before the start of the COVID-19 pandemic, I brought up to an Elder my discomfort even with being called that. The Elder explained to me that *Knowledge Keeper* isn't really the best term, either, for it almost sounds like you're keeping the teachings and lessons all to yourself. She said, "We are Knowledge Carriers. Your Elders shared their teachings with you, and it is now your job to carry them forward to share with others. You're not 'keeping' them, you're only carrying them for a time." This sentiment clicked with me, and it made me appreciate the role bestowed upon me in a different light.

I still see myself as *otâcimow*, a storyteller, sharing the words and thoughts gathered and lessons given to me by those who are not here to share it themselves, and I have an obligation to share those teachings through the medicine I carry, the medicine of words.

I do not claim to know the right answers to anything. I do not state that the words within this book are a truth above and beyond the words and truths of others who have come before me, or who will come after me. Only a fool claims to be the ultimate source of knowledge on a subject.

These words are simply my thoughts and feelings, as well as the teachings I was given, which I hope that I have shared in an entertaining, educational and respectful way, fully aware that how I see the world is vastly different from others, and in acceptance of the fact that others may take umbrage or disagree with what I have to say. There is no more malice in my words than there is in my heart or mind, and to carry the gifts I have been given, and to provide the knowledge that has been asked of me, I cannot live with malice or avarice in my life. This is not *miyo-pimâtisiwin*, this is not the good way of living life. To be given such things as an eagle feather, or to be given the responsibility of becoming a drum keeper or pipe carrier, or to be looked upon as a Knowledge Carrier, it is acknowledged that you already have begun, or it is expected that you will immediately begin, to change the way you live your life, in harmony, respect and peace with the Earth and those with whom we share it. This goes with what we say, as well. We must take responsibility for our words, and we must accept responsibility for the actions and reactions that our words cause. Mindfulness is required at all times.

To share one's words is to make one vulnerable. You open yourself to criticism and ridicule. This is the gamble all writers must take, sharing emotions with complete strangers and people who thought that they knew you. As someone who has personally suffered gaslighting many times in my life, I have had to learn who is a safe person and who is not. Tragically, those who should be considered safe in our society are often the ones who caused harm in the first place. This has led me to set new boundaries that are painful to implement, but these boundaries are often necessary for my own mental safety and security. This goes with this writing, as well. This must be said before I proceed further.

I keep my circle sacred, healing and small, minutely small. If you wish to be in my circle, or remain in my circle, then you must understand that there are things that are unquestionable and non-negotiable.

You will not question my loyalty, nor will you question my honesty. You will not question my intelligence, nor my integrity.

Above all, you will never question my trauma. I do not care if you were standing there beside me when it happened, my trauma is above speculation, and it is not for scrutiny or debate. It is my trauma, and I will choose to deal with it however I need to in order to heal.

If you cannot respect this, then you are not in my sacred circle. You are merely an acquaintance, even if you are blood.

I am very meticulous when it comes to creating a dedication for a book. It is something that I take great pains to ensure is meaningful, and that the work within stands in comparison and is complimentary to the person to whom the book is dedicated. It can be tricky.

Carrying It Forward

This book is dedicated to a role model of mine. I have very few remaining role models. The ones I once had have since proven themselves at best fallible and at worst downright horrible people. This person, however, is both an artistic and lyrical inspiration, as well as a testament to tenacity and perseverance in overcoming extreme obstacles.

When the rock group the Runaways disbanded in the late 1970s, Joan Jett struck out on her own and began a solo career. Seeking a deal with a record label, she was met with rejection not once or twice, but twenty-three times from the major labels. Undeterred, she paid for the album to be pressed and then began selling the album out of the trunk of a car. She never gave up her goal of having her work heard by the world, and in her determination to do so, she became an icon and a legend.

One of my dearest possessions is an autographed photo of Joan Jett I got somewhere along the line many years ago. I've seen her live twice, and both times she blew the main act off the stage.

So, to honour a true warrior who didn't let a thing like rejection bother her, I dedicate this book to Joan Jett, for being one of my last true heroes by being true to herself and her dreams. Thank you.

John Brady McDonald
Paddockwood, Saskatchewan, Treaty Six Territory
December 2021

The New North Territory

I wonder what my grandfather would think about this?

There is a map I once saw from the year 1900, showing the boundaries between the western Canadian territories prior to the creation of the provinces of Saskatchewan and Alberta in 1905. On this map, the area that is now Saskatchewan is divided into four distinct territories: the Districts of Saskatchewan, Assiniboia and Athabasca, and the western edge of Manitoba.

During this period, the capital city of the District of Saskatchewan was Prince Albert.

I was born in Prince Albert, Saskatchewan, at the beginning of the 1980s, one of the last ones through before they slammed the door on who gets labelled Generation X (though various individuals and websites say that I am actually a millennial). Aside from a few years living in Alberta, and a summer spent at university in England, my four decades upon this earth have always seen my mail delivered within

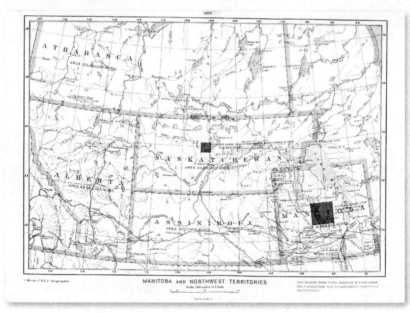

Map of Manitoba and Northwest Territories, 1900.
Courtesy of the University of Manitoba Archives and Special Collections.

an hour's drive of the city of Prince Albert. The city sits on the banks of the North Saskatchewan River, and – prior to the arrival of European explorers and missionaries, in particular a Scottish missionary named James Nisbet in 1866 – the area was known among my ancestors as *Kistahpinânihk*, which, when translated from Cree into English, refers to a meeting or gathering place. This was where we gathered and often wintered.

The North Saskatchewan River runs eastward, having cut a channel over the centuries that created the geographical sections by which the city has been divided. There is the Hill, bisected by Central Avenue into what is called the East Hill and the West Hill, and the Flats, also cut by Central into the

East Flat and the West Flat. Both East Hill and West Hill are often viewed as the "nicer" parts of town. The West Hill is home to large, some would say stately, character homes from Prince Albert's halcyon days in the early twentieth century, as well as newer homes often called McMansions. That being said, the West Hill was also the sight of the residential school attended by not only myself, but also my siblings, and my mother and her siblings.

The East Hill, once seen as the suburban dream of Prince Albert's wealthier families, has lost a bit of its lustre over the years, but still is considered the "nice" part of town, where the professionals – the doctors and lawyers and school principals – live. The outer edges of both the East and West Hills have seen expansion over the past few years, with fancy cookie-cutter houses backing onto bare empty fields that used to be a lot closer to the centre of town.

Down the hill to the north are the Flats. The East Flat, though it often goes unspoken, is felt to somewhat be the "blue-collar" area of town. The houses and neighbourhoods down in that part of the city were once seen as nice, respectable and clean, but are slowly becoming less desirable as time goes on. Early in the city's history, the East Flat was actually two smaller settlements – East Prince Albert and Goshen – that were gradually absorbed into the city as it encroached ever outward.

The West Flat, for as long as I can remember, has always been the ghetto, the 'hood, the poor and dirty part of town. It is seen as the roughest part of the city – home to gangs, to violence, to drugs and to abject poverty. Derelict homes stand boarded up beside slum dwellings that will soon be boarded up. It is where I was born and raised.

Between these areas, north-south along 15th Street and east-west along Central Avenue, lie commercial areas that somewhat act as a buffer zone. The original main commercial area of the city was River Street, which ran parallel along the river. It was replaced in the 1900s by Central Avenue, which was the bustling downtown area for decades. By the 1970s, this had moved to 2nd Avenue West. Today, the main commercial area of the city is along 15th Street West, now known as Cornerstone. This is where you'll find the big box chains, the restaurants, the banks and the clothing stores. Now, the downtown area of Prince Albert, with its Edwardian brick storefronts along Central Avenue and River Street, is populated by the multitudes of Prince Albert's homeless population, who congregate along the riverbank, sleep in doorways and under stairs in -40°C weather, and are derided quite harshly by many in the city.

Keep in mind that all of this exists solely on the south bank of the river. Once you cross the Diefenbaker Bridge heading north, the northern boreal forest pretty much starts at the water's edge on the north bank. To the north of the river, you will find the suburban areas of Red Wing, Nordale and Hazeldell, and, heading farther north for about forty kilometres, farmers' fields right up to just past the village of Christopher Lake. The tree line, however, starts at the north bank.

As the main industry at the time was the pulp and paper mill to the north of the city, the ever-present smell of my childhood was the acrid, sour stench of the papermaking process emanating from the mill. It is a smell every kid who grew up in a paper mill town will recognize. As the mill closed down over a decade ago, that smell has been gone for a long time.

The city has labelled itself "The Gateway to the North," as it is the last major community one passes through by automobile before venturing north across the North Saskatchewan River, then on along Highway 2 to the community of La Ronge and into the boreal forest. There is another northern route, Highway 155, that will take you as far as the northern community of La Loche along the western side of the province, but only Highway 2 is a direct shot north, more or less, from the US border.

To put it all into perspective, Prince Albert is, by car, approximately 2,300 kilometres from Toronto, 1,700 kilometres from Vancouver and 600 kilometres north of the United States border.

As a result of its location – being the third largest city in Saskatchewan and a minor metropolitan centre on the very edge of civilization, as it were – Prince Albert still retains its traditional role as a gathering place. It is home to a largely transient population, with people and families venturing forth periodically from northern communities and First Nations for extended periods of time, before returning to homes in the north. As of this writing, the population of Prince Albert and area sits at somewhere between thirty-six thousand and forty-three thousand people.

Summers are short here, and winters are long and cold, minus twenty to minus forty degrees Celsius cold, for days on end. If you think of the classic Canadian winter, you can imagine Prince Albert from November to April.

Prince Albert is also known as the "City of Jails." Within the city boundaries can be found a federal penitentiary, a provincial correctional centre, a women's correctional centre, a young offenders centre and a healing lodge, as well as the local RCMP and city police holding cells. There is an urban myth, though often disproven, that by virtue of either a coin toss or a belief that it would create more jobs or revenue, the city of Prince Albert chose to be home to the federal penitentiary rather than the University of Saskatchewan, which went instead to the city of Saskatoon.

I used to theorize that when you looked at these two cities, their respective institutions reflected the attitudes of the citizens (or denizens) of each city. Saskatoon, with the academic and intellectual heft given to any university town, benefits from the fact that institutions of higher learning usually foster the expansion of one's mind and view of life. Logic would then dictate that the surrounding community would also nourish a similar mindset and way of life, and in fact Saskatoon is home to prestigious and acclaimed modern art galleries, a symphony orchestra and world-class scientific and technological laboratories.

Prince Albert, with its major industry being the incarceration of other human beings, is vastly different. When one of the major employers in town is an institution that works on the limiting of one's freedom and abilities, that mentality also filters down to the populace. Prince Albert is a very cold place, and not just temperature-wise. It is a hard place, lived in by harder people. Racism, addiction, gangs, desolation and despair run rampant, though, for a long time, it was rarely spoken about or addressed publicly. Now, response wavers between begrudging acceptance, unabashed pride, cries of "everything going to hell" or calls to take the law into one's own hands, and the rare people who still retain that spark of belief that things can get better. There is very little to do in the city, unless you can afford a cabin on one of the many lakes to the north of the city, a boat to play on said lakes or snow-mobiles to, well, also play on said lakes during the winter. In fact, the major source of entertainment for the people of Prince Albert involves leaving the city for Saskatoon, an hour and a half south on Highway 11.

As an artist and writer growing up in P.A., as it is more commonly known, I can attest first-hand to the city's lack of cultural and artistic appreciation. Arts events are rarely attended by more than a dozen people – usually the same dozen people over and over again. While Saskatoon can boast literary events for hundreds, as of this writing Prince Albert no longer even has a bookstore.

Don't get me wrong, Saskatchewan as a whole and the major communities in it are all dealing with their own struggles with drug abuse, violence, racism, gangs and poverty. Prince Albert, however, has always been known as a violent city, even in Saskatchewan. Growing up, whenever someone in Saskatoon or Regina found out where you were from, it was not uncommon to be asked, "You're from P.A.? Have you ever stabbed anybody?" Prince Albert's recent notoriety from being fourth on *Maclean's* list of Most Dangerous Places in Canada in 2020 – it was sixth in 2019 and third in 2018 – has only added to the general malaise that many people feel about the city.

So, why do I stay? Why have I chosen to remain in this place for as long as I have? Why have I chosen to raise my children here and to live out my life? I have had many opportunities to live elsewhere, have been offered employment in places like Toronto, Vancouver, the United States and even London, England. I spent a few years living in Calgary, and I have travelled the world, far beyond anywhere I had ever expected to go growing up in poverty in one of "Canada's Most Dangerous Places." In an online post, where I was writing about Prince Albert and giving an honest description of my life here warts and all, pulling no punches, I jokingly questioned my sanity as to why I hadn't fled this place so long ago.

It's an odd thing: Many of the people I grew up with had done just that. They fled in droves, leaving this city behind and swearing upon all that is holy that they would never return. Within a few months, or a few years, they found their way back here. I did the same thing, choosing to settle on a few acres of land north of the city. Why do we do it? Is it solely about familial connections and the relatively low cost of living? Is it something in the water? Is it Stockholm Syndrome?

Perhaps it's a connection to a knowledge and set of experiences and lessons learned in what can often be the most brutal of climates, both literally and figuratively. Like soldiers in conflict, one gains a certain set of tools that is beneficial if one wishes to survive. When you grow up in P.A., you learn very quickly a set of street smarts and tactics that, perhaps, are only beneficial when you live here. Like an athlete relying on muscle memory, the lessons that come into play once you turn left onto Highway 2 as you exit Highway 11 from Saskatoon serve no real purpose anywhere else but here.

I guess, from personal experience, I stay because, simply, this is my home territory. This is the land my ancestors have lived on for thousands of years, and not in some intangible nostalgic way. My great-great-great-grandparents walked upon the same riverbanks that I do. They watched the same tumultuous collisions of ice that I have seen when the river breaks in the spring. They picked medicines and hunted in the same strands of trees that I do. They survived here, and so do I. The north is a land that can kill you should you choose not to respect it, and the people of the north are living testaments to resilience, tenacity and connection, yet that is something southern Saskatchewan seems not to fully understand.

In my 2021 poetry collection, *Kitotam*, I spoke about the suffocating feeling I get when I stand on the bald, open prairie of southern Saskatchewan, devoid of trees. It feels like being in a foreign land, alone, away from home. This all may be called *Saskatchewan*, but up north feels like a completely different country.

If anything, the COVID-19 crisis has shone a light on the seemingly divisive approach of southern Saskatchewan to the north: in 2020, as the number of cases increased in the north of the province, hospital visits for northerners to the south were denied and calls were made for northern people to be barricaded and prevented from travelling. There were even instances where businesses in Saskatoon and Regina posted signs that read NO NORTHERNERS ALLOWED. It's difficult for me as an Indigenous person not to look at this through the lens of racism, seeing as the population of northern Saskatchewan is almost exclusively Indigenous. While it did not appear outright as racism, one draws parallels between a sign saying NO NORTHERNERS and signs from the Southern United States in the mid-twentieth century saying WHITES ONLY. Meanwhile, the natural resources of the north are sent south to pay for hospitals to which we are denied access, and bridges and roadways are being built and rebuilt in the south while many communities in the north do not even have all-season roads, and the major highway to the north still only has one bridge to cross the North Saskatchewan River.

Add to this the isolation of living in the north, with little in terms of outside interaction, entertainment and even access to food devoid of the ridiculous markups in prices seen across the Canadian north, the suicides and the despair of our youth, the lack of employment opportunities in the north, and the outlook continues to dim, yet it still feels as if the southern part of the province continues to take and take, with little regard to the human costs. For example, in the summer of 2020, Tristen Durocher, a young man and renowned fiddler living in northern Saskatchewan, alarmed and saddened by the multitudes of young Indigenous people who were taking their own lives in the north, and appalled that the provincial government of Saskatchewan had recently voted down the adoption of the Strategy for Suicide Prevention Act, walked 635 kilometres from Air Ronge, Saskatchewan, to the provincial capital of Regina in order to raise awareness of the tragedy occurring in the north and, hopefully, to convince the government to reconsider the suicide prevention bill. When he arrived in Regina, Tristen set up a tipi, surrounded by the photos of those Indigenous youth who had committed suicide, on the grounds of the Saskatchewan Legislature, right across the street from the massive Legislature Building. There, he began a forty-four-day ceremonial fast, hoping to draw attention to the plight in northern Saskatchewan and hoping to connect with the provincial leadership to raise these concerns. He walked over six hundred kilometres in the hope that perhaps the Saskatchewan leadership would at least walk across the street and listen to him. Instead, the Provincial Capital Commission were called, as bylaw concerns were raised that he was illegally camping in a city park and destroying the grass. Tristen was continually harassed by Regina citizens who would have food delivered to him while he was fasting, and who threatened to pull down his tipi and remove him by force. He was even taken to court in an attempt to remove him from the grounds. After forty-four days, he ended his fast. Sadly, the obstacles and vitriol Tristen faced were nearly identical to those faced by those who participated in the Justice for Our Stolen Children camp, who also took to the grounds of the legislature in 2018 to protest the acquittals of the killers of Colten Boushie and Tina Fontaine, both Indigenous youth murdered by non-Indigenous men, as well as the systemic racism existing across the various provincial and federal systems in Canada.

Over the past few years, the idea of a return to territorial status for the northern part of Saskatchewan has, on an intellectual level, risen to become an idea worthy of more fleshing-out by a few armchair political pundits, such as myself.

First of all, a major acknowledgement must be given to the late writer Harold R. Johnson. In May of 2020, two posts he made on his social media regarding this notion created an amazing and convoluted discussion regarding the possible creation of a new federal Territory, and I acknowledge Harold for this.

Being a lifelong student of history, I began to imagine a scenario – but please note, this is NOT like the Wexit morons in Alberta who wish to secede from the country to save a dying fossil fuel–based industry and remove themselves from Canadian jurisdiction.

Think back to 1999. That was the year that the Territory of Nunavut came into being, splitting off from the Northwest Territories to become its own entity. The population of Nunavut is around thirty-nine thousand people, the Yukon is about thirty-three thousand and the Northwest Territories is forty-four thousand.

The city of Prince Albert alone had a population of forty-three thousand people as of 2019.

According to the 2016 census, the Indigenous population of Saskatchewan was listed as 175,015 people, around 16.3
percent of the population of Saskatchewan. Of that number,
114,570 people identified themselves as First Nations, around
65.5 percent, while the number of people who identified as
Métis was 57,880, or around 33.1 percent. The vast majority of
the people of northern Saskatchewan are Indigenous people
living in Indigenous communities on their ancestral land;
land that is always sitting in the sights of southern politicians
with thoughts of resource exploitation.

It is tempting: Northern Saskatchewan, returning to its
territorial status after 115 years, with the city of Prince Albert
as its capital. Electing people, not political parties and their
ideologies. The people of the north, not beholden to Regina
anymore, becoming a distinct voice in Canada.

As I first began to add my voice to this concept, I found it
interesting that the main issue brought up by this hypothesis
was the inclusion of Prince Albert. For many in the northern
part of Saskatchewan, Prince Albert and its surrounding area
is seen as part of the southern part of Saskatchewan, with
all of the issues that encompasses in the north. It is a fair
assessment. In spite of boasting that it is "The Gateway to the
North," Prince Albert is equally as guilty of the exploitation
of northern resources and people for southern means, and
the area surrounding Prince Albert is very rural prairie in
attitude and geography.

When I first started to give a bit more thought to the
scenario, I had envisioned the southern boundary of this
new territory to extend to Batoche, the spiritual home of the

Métis Nation, where, in 1885, Métis warriors under Gabriel Dumont and Louis Riel engaged the Canadian army in battle for the last time. I had included Batoche in an effort to bring in that important Métis community and to acknowledge the town's powerful role for the Métis people. To do this, however, would take up an enormous amount of prairie, and, like the area around Prince Albert, it tenaciously holds on to the Prairie mindset.

I then considered the role of the topography and the aspen parkland tree line as the natural boundary between the boreal forest and the prairie, so I moved the line north to the small village of St. Louis, which lies between Prince Albert and Batoche. It still seemed too far south, however.

Finally, I considered that final boundary of the boreal forest and the North Saskatchewan River, and the need for an economic and metropolitan hub, and I included Prince Albert, to meet those specific infrastructure needs.

It does lead to some deep discussions as to what constitutes *the north*: Is it a frame of mind? Is it geography? Is it history? It's all of the above, and we know that.

What I do know is this: I live on the very edge of the boreal forest. I have raised my children here, and I will continue to do so until my time is done.

My grandfather lived and died in the north, and he devoted his life to the cause of the Métis and First Nation communities and people of the north. Before I go further, I must admit that, in his later life in the 1950s and 1960s, my grandfather was employed as a uranium prospector for the Saskatchewan government and for private enterprises, searching for uranium deposits in northern Saskatchewan. These were the days of Project Plowshare, when the Americans thought that nuclear detonation could be used for peaceful industrial uses – the time of "Our Friend the Atom." My grandfather disappeared in 1967, long before the world realized the true impact of nuclear waste.

My grandfather was a Marxist socialist, who deeply believed in the empowerment of the Métis peoples and the unity of the working class. His core belief was that the Métis gain a rightful place at the table, as equals and as partners.

If the vast northern portion of Saskatchewan joined Nunavut, the Yukon and the Northwest Territories, would this provide the clout needed for a great Indigenous political renaissance? Perhaps.

Of course, this is armchair cartography at the moment, purely speculation.

But it certainly is appealing... Hypothetically.

Keep in mind, I'm just a simple historian.

The Educated Savage

I am an Indigenous man robbed of his ancestral words. My mother language was stolen from me one generation before I was born, as the residential schools beat it out of my mother and father. My world was one where I learned English, and whatever Cree words I learned piecemeal from my Cree grandparents were not nearly enough to become conversational, let alone fluent.

I was forced to learn this language, this English language, and I have learned it well. I have learned to create with it, I have learned how to construct worlds with it, espouse ideas and concepts and have educated conversations. Most of all, I have been able to take this language of the Colonizer, this foreign tongue, and I have been able to employ it to speak out against oppression and the illnesses of society. I have been able to advocate for those who have felt that they cannot speak for themselves. I have chosen to use this language and these words to protest injustice and tyranny, to sing the praises of those who have succeeded, to share the stories of others and, painfully, to speak for those who are no longer here to speak for themselves. I have stood at the microphone in the spotlight and I have spoken these words I was forced to learn before I could learn my own.

For all of this, I have been both lauded and mocked, awarded and ridiculed. I have spoken before thousands of people around the world, and I have sat in empty rooms where no one has shown up. I am grateful for those empty rooms and empty seats. They have taught me to be humble, and I have managed to retain my humility. I understand my responsibility to use these words not as a weapon, but as a tool; my responsibility to use these words as medicine and not as poison, and to always speak the truth, as best as I can. For this, I have been referred to by many things: a "credit to my race," a "well-read Indian," an "educated savage" and, for my ability to "code-switch," to make myself sound more palatable for white people, I was often called an "apple." I was red on the outside and white on the inside, trying to act like a white man.

I will never forget the first time that I ever sat down and composed something of substance. I was an angry teenager, deeply frustrated with the hand I had been dealt in life. One bitterly cold winter morning, as I stepped into the warmth of the school that would, in time, be my saving grace, I was taken and marched into a classroom. I was sat down at an ancient computer, a machine of which I had no knowledge nor inclination to use. The teacher opened the word processor program and left me alone in the room with only one instruction: "Write."

I stared at that beige keyboard, and, with only my two index fingers, typed out the first words I had ever written on a computer. "What the fuck am I supposed to write about?"

That first sentence opened the floodgates, and I began to unload years of pent-up emotions, experiences, abuses and pain, pecking away at that keyboard with my two fingers. All these years later, I still only type with two fingers. When the well had been emptied, I looked up and began to bawl uncontrollably. I collapsed into a heap on the floor, the sobs wracking me for what seemed like forever. When I finally looked up through bleary, reddened eyes, I was astonished to find that I had spent seven hours writing at that computer, alone, or completely oblivious to anyone who came into that room.

I began my career as the writer for an editorial column in a small local newspaper – in reality, an eight-page want ads publication that predated Kijiji and Craigslist. I was given close to carte blanche to write whatever I felt like speaking about, and, being a young, somewhat militant Indigenous man with loads of street life experience but little in the way of grace and tact, I did just that. I wrote about what was going on in my life and in my world. The first piece of mail I received after my first column was a single page, written on a typewriter and shoved through the door seam of that very same school where it all began. It was a page-long diatribe against Indigenous people, filled with racism and hatred, stereotypes and vitriol, which ended by accusing me of plagiarism, then the line, "I can't wait for your next pathetic attempt at writing." I was seventeen years old. I still have that letter in its original envelope.

I have written very little that I am truly ashamed of. As writers, we all have pieces we have written that perhaps embarrass us a little, perhaps written at a more naive, immature point in our lives and careers. But there is one work that I have all but disowned, and wish that I could go back and never write.

The poem was a long rant of sorts, a retaliation by a young and stupid man struggling with his own self-identity and subjected to prolonged bouts of lateral violence and feelings of persecution. I had written it out of anger, railing against a movement that I had wanted very much to be a part of, but to which I had been denied entry.

What should have been nothing more than a moment of catharsis ended up in a place where I had desperately wanted to be for so long – in curriculum. An open call for submissions to an Indigenous Literature textbook came across my desk, and, without thinking, I submitted this poem. To my surprise and eventual chagrin, it was accepted and published in the textbook.

It wasn't until years later that the gravity of what I had done finally dawned on me, but by then it was too late. The damage was done. What should never have gone to print is there, and I regret it every day. I occasionally, every now and then, find a small royalty cheque in my mailbox from it, rarely more than ten dollars. When they do come in, I cash it and usually give it all at random to one of the many homeless people on the streets of Prince Albert, often in the parking lots around the major supermarkets. If something has to come out of that piece, then let it serve someone else.

In my 2004 poetry collection, *The Glass Lodge*, I address some of the racial slurs to which I was subjected in my youth, one of which was the N-word, preceded by the word *Prairie*. It was a slur against Indigenous people I was called often in my youth, particularly in grade eight by a student who would greet me with it every other day, almost always with a "war whoop," his flat palm tapped rapidly over his mouth. I will never forget the sound of his voice, the way he said it, the inflection as that word, those two syllables, left his mouth. I wrote that poem while still in my teens, still remembering the taunts and bullying that finally built up into a confrontation where I was left as the one who "threw the first punch."

When the book went to print, the word was printed in its entirety. Whenever I performed the poem live, I would pause just before the word – saying, "Prairie," but not the following word. I would make an exaggerated gesticulation, allowing the audience to mentally fill in the blank on their own. In time, I omitted the whole phrase entirely. When the rights to the poem were reverted back to me after the book went out of print, the first thing I did was immediately delete the phrase entirely from the master copy, and should the book ever go back into print, it will do so without that phrase.

Even though it was something that I was personally called, early on, I no longer felt that referencing that fact was necessary. It remains a hurtful and devastating word to anyone who has been called it. As the world began to take greater notice of this word and, in particular, those who were saying this word, those who were allowed to use this word and those who were not allowed to use this word regardless of the context, I felt glad that I was, even in a small way, able to take a small step in stopping the perpetuation of this particular slur.

The written word was foreign to most of the Indigenous Peoples of the Americas. Ours is a tradition of oral story-telling, so the act of writing down words for posterity is a relatively new European introduction. Even the syllabics used by the Cree were created by a white man named James Evans in the 1840s, according to the overview of Plains Cree history from the Saskatchewan Indigenous Cultural Centre (previously known as the Saskatchewan Indian Cultural Centre). Ours was a process of listening to others and remembering. Making these words as I do is Colonization Incarnate. I have reconciled myself to this knowledge, and I will never shirk from it, for a very important reason. If what I say or what I write does anything to bring down those obstacles facing others as a result of colonization, then I will relish in the fact that I have done so with the tools thrust into my hands in childhood, forged to destroy my own language, only to be used against itself.

The West Flat

I am a West Flat kid. I was born in the West Flat area of Prince Albert, Saskatchewan, in the Holy Family Hospital, on a frigid winter's night nearly forty years ago. I spent, more or less, my first fourteen years of life in the West Flat, within those sixteen blocks between the Saskatchewan Penitentiary and St. Mary High School. Even the residential school where I spent many of my first eight years growing up, the Prince Albert Indian Student Residence, sat on a hill overlooking the West Flat. I learned many of my life lessons playing in the streets around Manville Bay and the rows of town-houses known as the Projects, in the playgrounds of Queen Mary Public School and the old St. Michael's Elementary, on the oiled gravel of 18th Street West. What pocket change could be begged, scrounged, bummed or stolen went into the cash registers and arcade machines of Buddy's Grocery, Dent's Laundromat, Westside Coin Laundry and Sylken Confectionery. My way of viewing the world, the survival skills I needed to save me time and again and the way I deal with the day-to-day issues of life: all of it can be traced back to my childhood as a West Flat 'hood rat. Every street, every alleyway, every building is burned into my mind, they are the rooms of my memory palace.

I cannot begin to speak about this portion of my life without addressing my time in residential school. I write this at a moment in time when many years of trauma among survivors is coming to the surface with the news that the graves of 215 children were discovered at the site of the Kamloops Indian Residential School in British Columbia. As I write this, I am mindful of what I am about to say, for I am in deep grief and mourning for those lost children, who today would be our Elders, our Knowledge Carriers and our leaders, but had it stolen from them.

My experiences in residential school are something that, until the 2008 apology by then prime minister Stephen Harper, I had never really acknowledged, let alone unpacked. I will never forget the day I watched the apology. It was June 11, 2008. I was working at that time as a frontline Youth Outreach Worker at the Youth Activity Centre, a free drop-in centre in the downtown core of the city of Prince Albert. I was doing some paperwork and quickly scanning the news sites for interesting topics to print out and use on a bulletin board. (This was all years before Facebook, so we weren't getting information in real time just yet.)

I saw the words "RESIDENTIAL SCHOOL APOLOGY" on the banner headline, and clicked on a link to a video on one of the national news sites.

As Harper began to read the apology, I felt my body grow cold and my extremities begin to tingle. I wasn't sure what was really happening to me, but I continued to listen.

As Stephen Harper said the words "Not only did you suffer these abuses as children, but as you became parents, you were powerless to protect your own children from suffering the same experience, and for this we are sorry," the tears overtook me, and I began to sob uncontrollably. I felt an arm around my shoulder and what I assume were some encouraging words, but there was no stopping the repressed memories as they flooded back.

I have always been aware that I grew up in residential school, and that both of my parents were residential school survivors. My father attended the residential school in Duck Lake, Saskatchewan, coincidentally also known as St. Michael's, and my mother attended what was known at that time as All Saints School, which in 1969 became the Prince Albert Indian Student Residence (PAISR). In 1982, for reasons I am not familiar with, the Prince Albert Indian Student Residence came under Indigenous operation, and title to the land was transferred to the Peter Ballantyne Cree Nation, and the school continued to operate until 1996–97. In the 1970s, my father began to work as a supervisor at "The Residence" as the PAISR was commonly known.

PAISR was unique among residential schools, as it did not consist of one building, but was a series of barracks-like buildings sitting upon what was originally an army camp. The student buildings, known as "cottages," were scattered across the site.

When I was four, our family moved into a suite the size of a hotel room in one of the cottages, and my father was in charge of supervising the students. This was residential school survivors continuing the cycle by supervising residential school students. I grew up in the PAISR, and so did my sisters. We were in Cottage 3 and Cottage 4. It was the same residential school my mother attended. Just to clarify: My maternal grandmother and all of her surviving children were in residential school, both of my parents were in residential school and my siblings and I were in residential school. Three generations of residential school survivors. My children are the first generation in four to have never seen the inside of a residential school.

When I heard about the discovery of 215 graves at the site of the Kamloops Indian Residential School in late May of 2021, I immediately went back to being five years old.

School photo, 1980s.
Author's photo.

I remember how there was very little to the south and west of the school in terms of structures. There was a farmhouse, the Victoria Union Hospital, a little bit of poplar bush and farmland, fields planted and harvested year after year. There was a lot of open space.

To drive past there now, it is drastically different. There are luxury condos, a somewhat gated community with what passes for mansions in Prince Albert and a gigantic multi-use recreational facility. Construction continues as the area develops. Yet, the cottages and buildings of the residential school remain, now part of, as I mentioned, the Peter Ballantyne Cree Nation urban reserve.

There are new buildings on the site, too, built on what was once grassy fields and open land, in the years since we left the school. The cottages and buildings there when I was growing up were not the same buildings as when my mom went there. A lot of shovels have gone into the earth around that place for a long time.

As time has gone on, and I've watched machinery dig and move earth in and out for new buildings in that area over the years, I always feel a cold chill go down my spine, and, in the back of my mind, I always wonder, "Are they going to find anyone buried there? Are there graves around the area?"

To say that the discovery in Kamloops is heartbreaking does not even come close. Two hundred and fifteen children – stolen, incarcerated, indoctrinated, abused and then forgotten for decades. In death, they continued to be victimized by the system: names lost, identities stolen, robbed of dignity. Families who never even learned what happened to their children. Children dying away from their parents, in an evil and traumatic location, with no one to help.

It took a long time for the major news outlets to share the story, but when they did, I knew immediately what I would find in the comments and reactions: calls to "get over it," and the Haha emoji. The underlying hatred and evil of it all still exists. The buildings of many residential schools might be long gone, but the mentality behind it still exists. There are still people in this country, in this province, in our communities, who want to see residential schools brought back.

It is the duty of those of us who survived residential schools, and those whose parents survived, to continue to remind the world of what happened to us, to ensure that it will never happen again. Like others who have survived genocide, we also bear the responsibility of sharing the story for those no longer here to speak for themselves. There are many things that I am not ready to talk about in great detail about what happened to me there. I'm sure that, given what is now known about what happened in the schools, conclusions can be drawn, but those responsible are now out of the hands of any justice that can be meted out, and one day I may discuss it further, but I am not ready just yet. I may never be.

In the intervening years since the 2008 apology, I have been somewhat hesitant to speak up and share my experiences. There are times when I continue to either downplay what happened to me or feel that it is not my place to speak, because, even after all these years, there's the fear that I won't be believed or accepted. It's a leap of faith and a testament of strength to those who can commit to paper or speak publicly about what happened to them in those schools. As I was not forcibly removed from a northern Indigenous community and kept away from my parents, in many eyes, I am not seen as a residential school survivor, though I experienced the same lack of cultural connection, trauma and abuse that the other students did. The fear of being called a liar or being gaslit is very strong, and it speaks to another cycle of trauma stemming from the genocidal and abusive practices of the residential school system – another form of silencing the truth about what happened.

It is very aggravating when people believe that the residential school system was a hundred years ago and many generations back, a distant point in Canadian history viewed only through old black-and-white photographs and grainy black-and-white films. Just to put things into perspective: a few months after I left residential school, the first episode of *The Simpsons* aired. When the last residential school closed, *Friends* was already into season 3, the Spice Girls released "Wannabe," the Backstreet Boys released "Quit Playing Games (with My Heart)" and the movies *Independence Day* and *Twister* were in theatres.

It was only twenty-five years ago. We are not all some long-forgotten black-and-white photograph. We are still here.

It wasn't until I spoke to someone who is not only a survivor themselves, but also a major national advocate for residential school survivors that I finally felt somewhat comfortable with saying I was a survivor. I explained to them my time there, and how I felt like I didn't have the right to speak about it, and how it felt like it didn't really happen to me. I finally just asked them, "Am I even considered a survivor? Does my story even matter?" I could hear the emotion in their voice as they finally provided the validation, and for the first time, I felt truly believed.

One of the statements often made by narrow-minded, often non-Indigenous individuals is "How long do Canadians have to apologize for what happened to Indigenous people?"

It is something I have heard quite often, especially around Canada Day 2021, as a movement arose for communities to cancel Canada Day festivities in solidarity with residential school survivors and to mourn the thousands of children who are almost certain to be found buried in unmarked graves at the sites of former residential schools. This question has always irked me, for it smacks of a petulant child whining, "Okay, I'm sorry, you happy now?"

When this question was asked for the umpteenth time online, in one of the horrible comments sections of a news article, I sat down with a notepad and began to write a list, which I then posted on social media.

It is as follows:

"How long do we have to keep apologizing for what happened?"
- when all Indigenous communities have clean drinking water and decent living conditions
- when Indigenous people are not seen as "getting handouts" or "begging for money" for seeking equality
- when Indigenous people are no longer told to "get over it" and "move on"
- when oil pipelines are no longer routed through Indigenous Territory
- when the majority of children in "Care" are not Indigenous
- when the majority of those incarcerated are not Indigenous

- when Indigenous Women and Girls stop disappearing and stop being murdered, and their killers stop going free
- when Indigenous youth are not driven into a life of gangs, addiction and violence
- when Indigenous people are no longer racially profiled and followed around stores
- when the blame for rural crime is no longer laid solely upon the shoulders of Indigenous people
- when Indigenous concerns and protests are actively and honestly acted upon, not met with the RCMP
- when there are no longer Angry or Haha emojis on posts concerning Indigenous issues
- when the mockery, disdain, hatred, vitriol and racism towards Indigenous people online stops completely
- when Indigenous people are fully and completely treated with respect, dignity and humanity
- when the perpetrators of atrocities against Indigenous people, from the Church to the farmer "defending his property," are brought to justice
- when Treaty rights and sovereignty are fully recognized, implemented and defended by all government agencies (federal, provincial, municipal and rural)
- when Indigenous voices are given an equal and recognized voice at the table

When can the apologies stop?

They can stop when people stop doing what they are supposed to be apologizing for.

The apologies can stop when it stops happening.

I made the caveat that this list was far from complete, and this list was shared over six hundred times within a few days of being posted. Other individuals have added their own "whens" to the list, such as the end of the forced sterilization of Indigenous women that has occurred recently, and the return of ancestral territory to Indigenous groups.

There is a photograph from a newspaper taken in the early 1990s of a procession of elementary schoolchildren following behind a Catholic bishop. It was posted on the Facebook page of the Prince Albert Historical Society, which holds a large part of the photo archive of the *Prince Albert Daily Herald* newspaper. The children have their hands raised in the air. This was the last day of classes at the old St. Michael's School, now the Bernice Sayese Centre. The procession is walking from the old school building to the new school, built a few blocks away. There is a kid in a black T-shirt in the bottom left corner of the picture. It is me. This was the school I had attended when I was growing up in residential school, and, after I had left the residential school, it was one of the schools I attended again. I had never seen this photo before. I was not expecting it. Colonialism is captured in this photo.

This school was a jarring, scarring place. This was the place where I was first punished for speaking Cree – sent out

Students leaving the old St. Michael's Elementary, 1992. The author is in the black T-shirt near the bottom left corner.
Photo from the *Prince Albert Daily Herald*, Prince Albert Historical Society E1000.

into the hallway or had to stay inside for recess with my head down on my desk. This was the first place, though certainly not the last, where I, along with other Indigenous students, on hot dry June days were mockingly invited to do a "rain dance" in front of the class.

I remember that I was in this school when the first water-slides were built in our city. They are still in operation, and, a few times, my wife and I have brought our family to the waterslides. Any time we go, my wife and kids will run off to play in the water and go down the slides, while I sit at a picnic table well away from the water, writing.

I've been many times over the years, but I never get in the water here...never.

I did once, though, very long ago. It nearly killed me.

This place opened sometime in the late '80s or early '90s, and class trips were a big deal.

It was 1990, grade four, and I was around nine years old. Having grown up in the poor part of town, with no access to a place to swim, I had never learned to swim. To this day,

I still really don't know how. This trip was my first time ever being in a swimming pool.

There are three big waterslides, along with a shorter "kiddie" slide.

I stood in line for the little slide, waited my turn, sat on the blue fibreglass edge and went down a waterslide for the first time in my life. When I went into the water, I fully expected to touch bottom, like the splash parks in the playgrounds. There was no bottom, though, and I kept going under.

I began to panic, thrashing and trying like hell to get out of the water, but all it did was make it worse. The gurgling of water in my ears was deafening, and I was terrified.

My mouth and lungs filled with water, and I began to sink down to the bottom.

I barely registered the arms of the lifeguard around me as they pulled me out. I coughed and sputtered for what seemed like forever. I was happy that I was soaking wet, so that no one could see how hard I was crying.

The teacher made me sit by a tree by myself for the rest of the visit. I sat there alone for three hours until it was time to leave. I never went back in the water. In fact, it was another twelve years before I ever stepped into another swimming pool, and that was with my wife. I'm still not comfortable with swimming pools.

This school was where I had Christian dogma forced upon me, and this was a school where I was bullied mercilessly.

The thing that stuck with me the most, however, was a painting. In the stairwell of this building was a large painting of St. Michael slaying the devil. St. Michael was this blond, blue-eyed man with his white foot on the throat of a dark-skinned devil. I would stop in the middle of the stairs and stare at this painting, terrified. I couldn't stop staring. I have included this painting a few times in some of the fiction I have written over the years.

The greatest day of my life was when I walked away from all spirituality and took back my life. I will never return to spirituality. To this day, I wonder what happened to this painting. Is it still in some storage room, collecting dust in the darkness? Was it also destroyed when the wrecking ball brought down the upper storeys of the building during renovations?

Today, the West Flat area continues to be known for the poverty, hopelessness and despair that seems to thrive within it. Gang activity and drug abuse have overtaken the streets where I once played, and the cost of purchasing a house in the neighbourhood can sometimes be nearly $200,000 less than a comparative house on the other side of town; the other side of town being thirteen blocks or so to the east or south. Nevertheless, it was my birthplace, and I hold the area deep within my heart with love and affection.

The West Flat is a tough place to live, and it produces some of the most resilient and resourceful individuals you will ever meet. As time goes on, it may seem that the West Flat is getting worse and more dangerous. Perhaps, or perhaps it is just the world catching up with the place. One thing is for certain: I will never be ashamed of being a kid from the West Flat.

Not THAT John A.

There is a slightly crude joke that is often told at family and traditional gatherings. It tells of a father and son who were both, in their salad days, depending on who's telling the joke, either champion powwow dancers or singers. They also both excelled at what is known within Indigenous circles as "snagging" – hooking up with a romantic partner for a relationship of varying lengths of time.

The son, after attending a powwow at a named community, falls in love with a beautiful young woman. (The joke is always told in a heteronormative fashion.) He takes her home to meet his parents, introducing her to his mother first, who approves of the young woman.

When the young man introduces the girl to his father, the father asks the young woman her name, how old she is and where she is from. When she replies, the father asks, "Do you know so-and-so?" to which the young woman replies, "Yes, that's my mother." The father shakes his head apologetically to his son and tells him that, as a young man, he was at a powwow at that community back then, and that he met a girl there, and that one thing led to another, eventually revealing that this young woman might in fact be the son's sister.

Dejected, the young man breaks it off with the young lady, and then goes off once again to seek his true love.

The pattern repeats itself season after season, with the young man bringing home a young lady he met at a powwow in some community (the teller of the joke will often supply names of real Indigenous communities), only to discover that his father may possibly be the father of the young lady.

Defeated, the young man breaks down and laments the scenario to his mother, complaining that "every time I meet a nice girl and want to marry her, Dad's been there and snagged her mom and that could be my sister!"

The mom, turning to her son, tries to console him, and says, "Don't worry, my boy. That's not your dad."

My name at birth really and truly was John A. McDonald. When people found out that I, as an Indigenous artist and activist and one who survived residential school, happened to share the name with Sir John A. Macdonald, the first prime minister of Canada, the man who fought Louis Riel and who believed in Manifest Destiny, the architect of the residential school system and the man whose actions brought despair, colonization and death to my people, they either assumed that it was not my real name, and/or would ask me the same thing:

"Why the fuck would your parents name you that?"

My father's name was John Baptiste McDonald. I only knew my father for the first eight years of my life. He committed suicide in January of 1990. I have lived my life five times longer without him than I did with him.

It was my father who named me John A. McDonald, after himself, though I will never know why he chose to give me a middle name different than his own.

For a long time, I tried to soothe the situation over with humour. I would joke that when I was born my father reached into his pocket and named me after the first thing he found, which was a ten-dollar bill with a picture of John A. Macdonald, and if he was ten dollars richer, and had a twenty-dollar bill with the image of the Queen, my name would be Elizabeth.

I have no memory of my father ever being referred to by his first name. My mother called him "Yogi," pronounced "YOU-ghee." I learned that as a child and in our home community of the Muskeg Lake Cree Nation he was called "Sabachease," pronounced "SAII-bah-Chease." I've since discovered that this is an old Michif/Cree way of pronouncing the name "John Baptiste." Subsequently, growing up, I was never referred to by first name in my family, both closely and in my extended family, only by second name. Theoretically, this was done, as per my mother, to avoid confusion between my father and I whenever someone would call out "John." However, as he never used his name in our family setting, this makes no real sense. To this day, many members, if not all, of the family who knew me as a child continue to refer to me by my former middle name, which was "Adrian."

I had not used my former middle name since I was a child. During my childhood, I was teased and bullied relentlessly about it by my peers. As I was a child when the film *Rocky* was released, I endured endless taunts in exaggerated impersonations of Sylvester Stallone calling out to his wife. I was also often taunted with the name "Adrian Adonis," who was a wrestler that performed in an exaggerated, effeminate, stereotypically homosexual manner, which, in the 1980s, was considered the worst thing you could be as a man or a boy. This was meant to be demeaning, embarrassing and shameful. This was when I was at a point in my life when I was just beginning to explore my sexual identity, just beginning to notice both boys and girls as more than just friends, and being labelled a "fag" and being called by the name of someone who "acted like a fag" added to the trauma that I attached to it. My name would be said in public or by a teacher, and I would die a little bit inside each time, cringing as if it was a knife being stabbed into my heart.

I was around twelve years old when I made the conscious effort to assert that I was to be known by my first name, and that I would no longer go by my middle name. By this point, my father had been dead for four years, and I was beginning to take greater control of my identity and my personal being, as well as beginning to deal with the bullying and harassment of my youth.

I began to deflect the anger that I held towards my name at my father, who had given me the name in the first place. There were plenty of other reasons I had for being angry with him, but the anger towards him for giving me that name was misplaced. It should have gone towards the bullies and homophobes who used my own name as a weapon against me.

In my early years, I had no sense of the gravitas of the name that I carried, nor the connotations behind that "other guy" who shared it. I looked into it a few years back and, at that time, there were thirty-one other men named "John McDonald" in the province, sixteen of us who were named "John A. McDonald."

I had no knowledge of the emotional and traumatic baggage that came along with this name. At that time there was not the ardent push to bring to light the horrors of the past and the role Sir John A. Macdonald played in the creation of the residential school system. He was just a trivia answer or a history legend, and if anything was mentioned about him, it usually had to do with his substance abuse problem.

It wasn't until I was a little older, and the calls for the recognition of the systematic atrocities committed by Sir John A. Macdonald began to grow, that I started realizing the situation I was in regarding my name.

It started for me when I began a closer study of the 1885 Riel Rebellion and the execution of Louis Riel. As a Saskatchewan elementary school student, a class field trip to Batoche is somewhat of a prerequisite, provided your school is within driving distance. If not, then you learn about the uprising in social studies, usually around grade four. I learned of the vitriol and anti-Métis, anti-Catholic attitude Macdonald personally held, and when I heard his quote regarding the execution of Riel – "He shall hang, though every dog in Quebec bark in his favour" – I knew that I shared a name with someone who was not a pleasant person, to say the least.

As activists and warriors began to fight to have the truth of residential schools and the near genocide of Indigenous Peoples brought out into the open, and as the country began the long process of what would become the Truth and Reconciliation Commission, the narrative of Macdonald as a glorious Father of Confederation began to shift to the narrative of a tyrannical bigot who fought for and advocated for the complete genocide of my people. There was a sense of Indigenous people and our allies standing together to shine a powerful light on this little man who had wielded dangerous power and who was still being held up as a mythical, quasi-holy beacon of the country's birth by those who felt that we as Indigenous people needed to "just get over it and move on."

Of course, the irony that I, a residential school survivor, shared a name with one of the architects of the residential school system was not lost upon me. I decided to add my voice to the struggle, hoping to stand and be counted in order to make a change.

What I discovered early on, however, was, frankly, people thought I was full of shit. People didn't believe that this was actually my name, and thought that I was falsely using the name "John A. McDonald" in some sort of twisted way of inserting myself into the narrative. Then, when I would state that, yes, I was indeed an Indigenous person named John A. McDonald, there were people who, because I am light-skinned, didn't believe that I was Indigenous and began berating me and attacking me for "pretending." Then, when I spoke out against the abuse I was suffering, people didn't believe that I was being attacked! The amount of gaslighting that went on was insane, and it took energy away from the issue we were trying to bring to the forefront, which was the treatment of us as Indigenous people by a man who should not have schools and streets and buildings named after him.

Because of this, I had given serious consideration to changing my name. I had spent nearly thirty years being attacked, bullied, belittled and mocked for a name I never asked for, and, like I did as a child, I was fully willing to carve out a new destiny and identity for myself, perhaps legally changing my name to the Nêhiyawak name I was given. I had even gone so far as to request the forms to do so.

One old John A. McDonald with another old John A. Author's photo.

However, for the longest time, I didn't. There are many reasons: by this point, I was already established professionally as John A. McDonald, and I was well known by my name. As well, I was married, and my wife and children share my surname, so it would not be fair to them to abandon the name and leave them saddled with it.

There was one very important reason why I never changed it, however, and it overrode everything for me.

In 2018 my children and I were officially transferred from the Mistawasis First Nation to the Muskeg Lake Cree Nation.

When I was born, I was registered as a member of the Muskeg Lake Cree Nation, my father's home community. I was a band member there until 2001 when my mother, sister and I transferred to my mother's home community, the Mistawasis Cree Nation (now known as Mistawasis Nêhiyawak). We had transferred because, at that time, there was a greater familial connection to my mother's home community than there was to my father's home, and when my children were born, they were also registered with Mistawasis.

When my father's brother, my uncle Emile, passed away around ten years ago, I attended the funeral. It was then that I noticed that the McDonald surname was quickly disappearing from the reserve. There did not seem to be many McDonalds left. I saw that our family lineage was withering, and that a time might come when there was no more family left with the last name of McDonald.

I have always had a deep connection with Muskeg Lake and I wanted my children to have a better chance at being accepted by their home community. We never really felt accepted or welcomed by my mother's home community. It always felt like we were outsiders, like we didn't belong. I don't know why, but I know it deeply hurt and still does to this day. To have grown up without that sense of community acceptance made me want it desperately.

I wanted my children to be acknowledged and accepted as Nêhiyawak, in spite of being light-skinned. I also wanted my children to know what it is like to have their home community proud of them and not treat them like less than because they are off-reserve. Muskeg Lake had always honoured and respected me. When I went to Cambridge on scholarship, Muskeg Lake was proud of me and helped me with funding.

I remember the first Treaty Day celebration we attended on the reserve after the children and I transferred back to Muskeg Lake. The first person I saw that day was Chief Kelly Wolfe, a veteran of the War in Afghanistan. The first words out of his mouth when he saw us were "Welcome home." It feels wonderful to have a supportive home community, and to be acknowledged as part of that community. It is home territory, and it is the land where my father, my uncles and aunties, my cousins and my ancestors lie buried.

I knew that to change my name completely would be a dishonour to those ancestors who came before me.

I tried my best to rise above this name I was saddled with; to make it my own and be great in spite of it, and I thought

The McDonald family with Chief Kelly Wolfe, Muskeg Lake Treaty Day 2019. Author's photo.

that I would continue to use it, and I would continue to find a way to use it for something positive.

Then an interesting situation developed around 2018. Across the country, there were calls for municipal, provincial and federal governments to remove the name of Sir John A. Macdonald from public buildings and infrastructure, as well as the removal of the numerous statues devoted to the man across Canada. In 2018, the Royal Canadian Mint began circulating new ten-dollar bills featuring the image of Viola Desmond, a Black woman from Nova Scotia who, in 1946, stood up to segregation by refusing to move from her seat in a segregated movie theatre. Her image replaced that of Sir John A. Macdonald, who had been on the ten-dollar bill for nearly fifty years. It was the beginning of the tide turning for that other John A.

As news articles and social media posts began to appear around the statues and the ten-dollar bill, people began to share these stories, adding their own opinions and thoughts, including people on my various friends lists. However, when they would go to write the name "John A. Macdonald," almost 80 percent of the time they would spell it "John A. McDonald," and, inevitably, I would be tagged in their posts.

At the height of the calls for the removal of the statues, my phone was constantly notifying me that "So-and-so has tagged you in a post," and, for about a period of three weeks, the tags were solely as a result of the misspelling of the surname. I finally made an appeal online for people to double-check and make sure that they were spelling the name correctly before posting, and I found myself stating, "I'm not THAT John A."

Eventually, my appeals were discovered by news outlets across the country, and, for a time, I was sought out by national media outlets who wanted to hear the story of the Indigenous guy named John A. McDonald, and know my thoughts on the issue surrounding the statues. I was finally provided the chance to share on a larger platform what it meant for me to have this name, and to have my feelings about it be taken seriously and not as some form of comedic fodder.

Every reporter would inevitably ask my opinions on the matter, and whether or not I agreed with the removal of the statues and the names. It was easy to determine rather quickly by how they asked me whether the reporter saw it as a positive step towards reconciliation or as a step towards what they saw as Cancel Culture. You could hear it in the cadence of their voice, either the faint hint of dismissal or the actual honest belief in the story, and in the way they posed the question. I was asked it in two different ways: either "What are your thoughts about the statues/calls to bring down the statues?" or "Do you think that bringing down the statues is right/wrong/erasing history?"

I always answered the question the same way. I would reply, "As a historian, I can tell you that there is no lesson that can be learned from them other than nineteenth-century bronze sculpture technique." When pressed on what to do with them, I would state, "For years, it was believed that the Russian guns and cannons captured by the British during the Crimean War were melted down, and the metal used to create the Victoria Cross, the highest military award in the British Empire. This has since been proven to be inaccurate. That being said, I feel that a similar thing could be done with these statues. They should be taken and melted down, and the metal used to create a commemorative medal to all of us who survived the horrors of the residential school. There should be enough statues of Sir John A. Macdonald out there to make eighty thousand medals. Perhaps each medal could say, 'He tried to steal every bit of you. Here is a little piece of him. You survived, he didn't.'"

These moments brought back memories of a time when I was still a young, politically energized, self-professed scholar trying my best to be a rabble-rouser. When I was around nineteen or twenty, I had begun to look into an odd historical scenario that eventually turned into a much deeper rabbit hole than I had originally anticipated.

I had noticed that on the application form for a Canadian Social Insurance Number, required by individuals in order to work in this country, there was a strange thing. If you look at section 10 of this form, you will see "APPLICANT'S STATUS IN CANADA," and you are given the chance to select one of five choices. The first two selections are as follows: "CANADIAN CITIZEN" and "REGISTERED INDIAN."

Now, as I had understood it, the *Oxford English Dictionary* defines the term *treaty* as "a formal agreement between two or more countries." Thus, by virtue of Treaty, Indigenous bands could be considered, for all intents and purposes, sovereign nations within the confines of Canada. Therefore, Indigenous people who have Status are "not" Canadian citizens, though we are still entitled to all rights and freedoms, and subject to all laws and regulations as Canadian citizens. Now, while the British North America Act of 1867 transferred "Responsibility" of "Indian Matters" from the British to the newly formed Canadian government, the Indian Act refers to reserve land in this manner: "Subject to this Act, reserves are held by Her Majesty for the use and benefit of the respective bands for which they were set apart, and subject to this Act and to the terms of any treaty or surrender, the Governor in Council may determine whether any purpose for which lands in a reserve are used or are to be used is for the use and benefit of the band." By this definition, one could argue that Indigenous bands are, in essence, British colonies in miniature, controlled by the Crown "in the best interests of the Indians," because we apparently didn't know what was best for us after fifteen thousand years of successful and continuous existence on this land.

Prior to 1919, Canadian citizens were eligible to be awarded and honoured with British titles and appointments, such as knighthoods and peerages to the British aristocracy, including the Order of the British Empire (OBE). Canadians could be made barons, earls or lords in the British peerage system, and this rankled some of the early politicians in twentieth-century Canada who felt that this wasn't in line with notions of democracy and such. The 1919 Nickle Resolution eventually led to the prohibition of British honours being bestowed upon Canadian citizens.

There was a time when, for those of us with Indian Status to become "Canadian," we would have to go through a process called "enfranchisement," which means giving up all claims and rights as an Indigenous person provided under Treaty. For decades, enfranchisement was mandatory for any Indigenous person who wished to receive a university degree, become a doctor or a lawyer, or even vote. If you never became enfranchised, one could argue, you never became Canadian.

I felt that there was a strong argument that, by virtue of this and many other factors, such as the Indian Act, the Jay Treaty, the BNA Act and so on, there had to be a loophole available that would allow Indigenous People to, at best, be considered British subjects and receive British citizenship, or, at least, be exempt from the Nickle Resolution and be allowed to receive British honours.

The reason for all of this research? It seems silly now, when I think about it. I had decided that there was the slightest chance that I would be eligible for a knighthood, and thus I could actually assume the mantle of being "Sir John A. McDonald." In the naivety of youth, I had this notion that the irony of an Indigenous activist being named Sir John A. would be the ultimate slap in the face to the Establishment and to the colonial powers that be who still attempted to wield authority over us. I was mischievously plotting and planning what kind of troubles and demonstrative chaos I could cause with such a title. I had been mockingly called "Sir John A." my whole life, so why shouldn't I accept the title and use it to my own advantage?

I was in way over my head on this idea at the time, only scratching the surface and probably a page or two away from a bit of research that would scuttle the whole concept. I possessed neither the clarity nor the foresight to see what a fantastical pipe dream it was, but the idea died on the vine in the end. However, I do give that younger version of me credit for the diligent research he had done, considering the massive amount of personal issues I was dealing with at that time.

Looking back, I can now see it as a much-needed distraction from the internal chaos of a young man slowly coming to grips with addiction and transitioning from a traumatic youth to adulthood.

In 2021, the horror of graves at the Kamloops Indian Residential School was the straw that broke the camel's back. I knew, as I sat, curled up into a ball, the tears pouring out, that I could no longer bear the same name as what I like to call the Monster of Confederation.

When the Government of Saskatchewan announced that they would waive the fees for residential school survivors to legally change their names, I knew that this was the moment to make things right.

My name really was John A. McDonald.

For forty years, I bore that name. I carried the pain and shame of it, suffered teasing and bullying because of it, tried my best to use it in a beneficial way, only to have the pain continue, and, as a residential school survivor, have that name continue to cause pain in myself and other survivors. I have been embarrassed and humiliated by my name. I had never loved my name. It brought me nothing but pain.

That pain ended July 13, 2021. John Adrian McDonald died.

With the help of Eugene Arcand and the National Centre for Truth and Reconciliation, and with the blessing of my mother and my family, I legally changed my name. From here on in, both personally and professionally, my name is John Brady McDonald. I chose this name to honour my grandfather and hero, Métis leader Jim Brady, and to acknowledge my father, who was also John B. McDonald and a residential school survivor. I now have a name to be proud of.

The trans community uses the term *deadname* to refer to the name they were assigned at birth and no longer use when they have finally become who they truly are. I am not sure if the phrase applies in my case, but I would hope that, like the basic human respect that should be shown to trans women and men who are finally living their honest lives, you will also respect me and no longer use my deadnames – either

John A. McDonald or my middle name alone. I will no longer answer to them. And, if you're one of those people who say, "I'm still going to call you Adrian," then don't bother calling me.

Many statues of Sir John A. Macdonald have toppled over the years.

I have finally brought down one of my own.

When my last piece of ID with my new name arrived in the mail, I took all of my former IDs, including my old wallet, and buried them in my yard, deep beneath the earth. We held a goth funeral service for the name, and finally laid to rest, literally and figuratively, that name. Over the grave sits a marble headstone bearing a bronze plaque. It reads,

JOHN ADRIAN MCDONALD

1981–2021

THIS NAME LIVETH NEVERMORE.

I began this essay with the retelling of a joke. Now, as I wind down this tale, I am able to swing around full circle to it.

For my entire life, I had a deep and longing desire to discover the origins of the McDonald surname on Muskeg Lake. I knew that my paternal grandfather had the surname of McDonald, while my paternal grandmother had the surname of either Wolfe or Lafond, two of the earliest family names on the reserve.

I had spent several years going through census records and tracking down various documents, trying to determine when this Scottish last name first appeared in our Indigenous community.

I had always assumed that the McDonald name entered the community in the way that many European surnames entered Indigenous communities – a white person, unable to properly pronounce the Indigenous names of people, simply substituted their own surname in place of the "Indian name."

I had been attempting to discover our traditional family name, hoping that it might be an option for me when I was considering changing my name. As time went on, it also became an attempt to reconnect with my father's family and my ancestral connections there.

Finally, I felt that I had discovered the evidence that I had been looking for. I traced a Scots-Irish man named Alexander McDonald, who arrived in the area in the late 1800s and who had taken part in many negotiations with the Cree and Métis people who were there at the signing of Treaty Six. I felt strongly that this man was the first McDonald in the line. After years of genealogical and historical research, I had succeeded, and, with pride and confidence, I presented my discovery to my mother.

Her response? "You know that your dad's dad wasn't his real dad, right?"

It turns out that the man I knew as my paternal grandfather, a man named Jerimiah McDonald (I say "knew," but who in fact died a few years before I was born), had raised my father as if he was his own son, and, in fact, my father's biological father was a man from my mother's reserve.

I sat in stunned silence, as I watched the carefully constructed lineage I had "rediscovered" evaporate before my eyes. I suddenly remembered the joke about the powwow singers, and I began to laugh.

As Indigenous people, we constantly seek connections, constantly search for the ties and lines that unite us. When you have a connection to a community, you play the game of "Who's your mom? Who's your grandmother? Oh, I knew her!" and that game will lead to stories and knowledge about your family that is wonderful, confusing and never dull. It is our strongest bond, that line of family, and it is the backbone of our resilience. No matter what, it is the one constant source of our strength, and it is something that, in spite of how hard that other John A. tried to destroy us as a people through his genocidal policies and his hatred, he could never break. We are strong, because those who came before us were strong, and they showed the path and provided the lessons and teachings necessary in order for us to continue, in spite of the pain, in spite of the death, in spite of the attempts to shame and humiliate, to be stronger, more determined and relevant.

Ruminations on England

An all-too common post on social media shows a remote, desolate cabin, ridiculously extravagant, perched either in a majestic forest or along the shores of a gloriously beautiful lake. With it comes the question "Could you stay here for a year without...," then a list of various first world "necessities," such as internet access, etc. Conveniently absent from these tourism dreams, of course, are the givens that are part and parcel of that type of existence, such as the horrendous infestations of mosquitoes and blackflies; the knowledge that a major portion of said year would be spent in the depths of winters so brutal and treacherous that you will quickly find yourself drawing parallels to Stephen King's *The Shining*; the massive coordinated logistical effort in acquiring, transporting and storing even the most basic provisions to meet the needs of anyone living that isolated for an extended period; and, finally, the knowledge that if you are hurt, or you are in trouble, it is going to take a very,

very long time for help to arrive, if it arrives at all. Granted, it is mere internet fluff – a generic post shared for momentary what-if enjoyment, not meant to be read into too deeply.

My brain, however, doesn't work that way, and I find myself constantly picking apart things like this, filtering them through reality and pragmatism. Perhaps it makes me an old curmudgeon, though I do not begrudge those who post it. I simply evaluate the posts based on practicality. Perhaps it is the wisdom gained by going without for so long and surviving on so little that makes me suck the life out of things like this. I do not know, but I generally try to keep it to myself; there's no sense in raining on someone else's parade.

This is not to say that I do not indulge in idle fantasies and what-ifs. I would be a fool to say that I have never dreamed of what it would be like to win the lottery or suddenly have the financial wherewithal to drastically alter my current state of affairs. My dreams, however, seem to deviate rather drastically from those around me. Whereas co-workers and family members dream of tropical beaches, Mexico, Cuba and Hawaii, or spend Easter breaks in Las Vegas, my "dream getaway," as it were, is more sedate. I have no desire for sand, surf or the Strip.

I see myself ensconced in a small cozy cottage in an idyllic English countryside, the rain pattering down upon the cobblestones, as a warm fire burns in the hearth. There is a cup of tea at my side, and a stack of books beside me from the local village bookstore. When the rain stops, I shall perhaps climb aboard my bicycle and ride the country lane to the train station, where I will travel to some quaint little university town to listen to a lecture, perhaps visit the local pub, then venture off across the moors or the footpaths of the Home Counties.

I know damn well that my vision of an England such as this is as fantastical and unrealistic as the posts about the cabin. Having lived there for a time, and having connected with others who are either from there or currently live there, this bucolic vision of a rural idyll is far from reality. In England, they refer to it as a "chocolate-box" vision of the UK, stemming from a time when Cadbury would use such imagery in their packaging. To some, it is as close to reality as the "igloos, dogsleds and red-coated Mounties" stereotypes of Canada.

As an Indigenous person who has borne the brunt of colonization my whole life, it may seem odd or contrary to speak in loving terms about the home base of imperial greed and power, the cornerstone of colonization. Indeed, there are many times when I myself question it.

I cannot deny that I am a product of colonization, and that this land as it is right now is still bound to the effects of that colonialism. Those colonial links between Canada and England must be acknowledged, in terms of the effects on my people. The horrible pain of colonization cannot be overstated. The trauma of colonialism remains with us to this day, and great strides taken by those of us who have survived residential schools and the cultural genocide to bring our Indigenous heritage and way of life back to the forefront must never be forgotten. We as Indigenous people continue to move forward in spite of the attempts to destroy us. We are still here. Nevertheless, it is in my DNA. I have ancestral blood from Britain as close as my great-grandfather, born in Ireland, and I still have distant cousins in Scotland. Many Indigenous people have similar ancestors in their heritage, the names of white trappers, prospectors, fur company factors still common in the west: McKenzies and Isbisters and McKays and Cooks and Halketts and Ballantynes and many others. One must also acknowledge that many Indigenous people have ancestry from across the pond as a result of having it violently forced upon them, and one must be mindful of the connotations of such.

My Nêyhiyawak *nimosôm nitanskotapan* (great-great-great-grandfather) signed Treaty with the British Crown.

My Nêhiyawak and Métis grandfathers served and trained in England during the Second World War, prior to the D-Day invasion.

I lived and studied in England, loved every minute of it, and they remain some of the happiest days of my life. I have stood in the teeming, soaking English rain, my bare feet upon the soil, staring into the sky like Tim Robbins in *The Shawshank Redemption*, the salty scent of the sea air filling my lungs. I have walked along country lanes and watched the pastoral English countryside fly past as the train I was on sped north to the Scottish border.

I have walked through ancient streets and been inside majestic buildings that were built centuries before the English even set foot on Turtle Island. I have stood beside Roman ruins and Viking settlements, and I have held Plantagenet artifacts from the Wars of the Roses in my hands, artifacts from a time when Henry the Eighth was a little boy. I have been fortunate and privileged in this, and I recognize the privilege that I was afforded the opportunity to experience England in person. I love British literature, British television, British history and British humour. I can watch *Antiques Roadshow*, *Midsomer Murders* and BBC documentaries for hours. My bookshelves dip under the weight of British books.

I still dream of immigrating to England, to some quaint little English village, and opening up a tea shop or bookstore.

There are times when I walk through an older building here in Canada, and the smell of age will hit me, for it is the scent that permeates so many of my fondest memories of "over there," for the rooms where I lived and the halls in which I studied bore similar scents and smells, and, without fail, I find myself reciting under my breath the Robert Browning poem "Home-Thoughts, from Abroad."

O, to be in England
Now that April's there,
And whoever wakes in England,
Sees, some morning, unaware.

Yes, it does feel hypocritical to be fighting for decolonization for Indigenous people, while at the same time extolling the virtues of the land so far away.

Perhaps it is the instinctual connection to ancestral land, an attraction to long dormant molecules of the stuff that makes us who we are, which leaves me yearning for my other ancestral soil. Do the two cancel each other out? No, I cannot let it.

It is upon me to rectify the two within me: the decolonized Indigenous warrior and the anglophile-by-choice.

As in most things, the duality of this phrase reflects the situation at hand.

Can one be decolonized yet still be an anglophile?

Big Shoes to Fill

At the site of the annual Back to Batoche festival sits the Métis Veterans' Memorial Monument. It is a beautiful semicircle of black stone obelisks, bearing the names of thousands of Métis veterans, from 1885 to today.

This monument is designed in such a way that one cannot simply look for a loved one's name either alphabetically or by which war they fought. The names are in no order – and to be able to find your loved one's name, you have to read and acknowledge every name on the obelisk. No rank nor fame places anyone above anyone else – Louis Riel and Gabriel Dumont are scattered in among the names.

Inscribed on the stones are many of my relatives. When I first visited the site after the memorial was erected, I meticulously scanned each name, looking for ones I recognized. There was one name, however, which I had hoped to find above all others – that of my maternal grandfather.

I was actually blessed to have two maternal grandfathers, both of whom played key roles in my development as an adult.

The man I knew growing up as "Grandpa" was a man named Terrance Bear. He was my step-grandfather, who had raised my mother as if she was his very own daughter. Grandpa Terrance was a farmer, a member of what was once known as the John Smith Indian Reserve, now known as the Muskoday First Nation. Grandpa Terrance had been, as family lore goes, on his own since he was a young boy in the early twentieth century, working for various farmers in the area around the reserve.

In 1943, when he was already in his forties, Grandpa Terrance enlisted in the Canadian Army to join the war effort. He became a sapper, equivalent with a combat engineer in the US Army, in the Royal Canadian Engineers. He was sent overseas, and he landed on Juno Beach some time shortly after D-Day.

Whereas most of the men who landed on that beach were barely old enough to be called "men," my grandfather was well into being middle-aged. He was the same age I am right now, at the time of this writing, with a good knowledge of the world and what it can entail. My grandpa saw action across Europe until the end of the war.

There is a glass display case hanging on the wall above my desk as I write this. Inside are the medals Grandpa Terrance received for his service in the Second World War. They are not medals awarded for a single heroic act or moment of bravery, but they represent the service he provided at a time when it was needed the most.

When I was a child, those medals sat in an old steamer trunk he had, wrapped in an ancient paper towel and nestled inside a worn cardboard box that once held Pot of Gold chocolates. Whenever my grandpa needed to go into that trunk, the box would be casually pushed to the side. He never opened the box himself, and whenever the box was opened, be it by my grandmother or someone else, I remember that my grandpa was never in the room. It seemed like the medals didn't exist to him, or, if they did, they were meaningless trinkets that were sometimes in the way of other, more important things.

After my grandmother's death in 1990, my grandpa left his home on the reserve and lived first with my older sister, then later with my mother, my younger sister and me. I often sat alone with him, watching wrestling or hockey on television, most of the time in silence.

I do not remember when he first began to share with me his wartime experiences. Perhaps something on television had triggered the conversation, a commercial or news story regarding veterans. Whatever it was, he decided to finally speak about what he'd experienced over there, and what he'd seen and gone through.

He spoke of watching the newsreels of Germans burning books in huge bonfires, something that he as a voracious reader was deeply bothered by. I remember him talking about walking through what had been a tulip field in Holland, and how the retreating Germans had turned the fields, by blowing dams and dikes, and by the treads of their mechanized vehicles, into sodden, mucky, muddy quagmires. He told me that he saw Dutch peasants on the verge of starvation rooting through the mud to find tulip bulbs in order to eat them.

He spoke of sitting one time beside a young soldier, talking and taking a meal, when he heard a soft plop and a splash of warmth on his face, as the young man beside him fell to the ground, shot through the head by the enemy. The warm splash on his face was the blood of the young man.

As a sapper, my grandpa's duties were, as he put it, "building bridges and digging ditches." He built field fortifications, created and repaired roads in front of the advancing columns, removed obstacles and essentially did the grunt work of building the infrastructure needed for the army to advance and meet its objectives.

He told me that he had entered the Bergen-Belsen concentration camp in 1945 as part of the Canadian-British liberation forces (the same camp where Anne Frank died). He could never properly put into words what he saw there in terms of the sights and smells. But he told me that, by the time he got there, after the main force had liberated the camp, they found thousands of bodies. Grandpa said they had to use bulldozers to bury the dead, because there were just so many bodies. One bulldozer would dig a long trench, then another bulldozer would push the bodies in. They did this day after day, he said, for nearly a week. He told me of the guards, who smugly shrugged at the mounds of corpses and, as my grandfather recounted to me, said, "What bodies? What Jews?"

I was a child when he told me these tales. They saddened him, and they horrified me. However, I noticed one thing in particular. He would stop speaking if anyone entered the room, and he would not begin again until they had left. While I'm sure he possibly shared his stories with my mother and my grandmother at some point before I was born, I had the feeling that I was one of the few people whom he had ever said anything to about it.

There were other tales in there, as well, pleasant ones, in fact. He told me of seeing the Eiffel Tower in Paris, and he spoke about the ship that brought him to Europe.

The one pleasant story I remember the best, however, was how his unit was massed on Blackfriars Bridge in London, and how they were inspected by no less a personage than His Majesty King George VI. Grandpa told me how he stared straight ahead, with the dome of St. Paul's Cathedral in the corner of his eye, and a church bell tolled ten in the morning softly somewhere behind him.

There is no known photo of him in his uniform or during the war, at least none that I have ever seen. I asked him one time about his uniform. I asked him what happened to it. "I burned it," he said, matter-of-factly. When I asked when, he said, "When I got back."

I have a memory, or at least I think it's mine. Perhaps I was told it as a kid and simply absorbed it into the sphere of Grandpa's story, I'm not sure.

Two representatives of either the Royal Canadian Legion or some other veterans' organization came to Grandpa's house on the reserve, to ask him if he wanted to march in an upcoming parade. My grandfather, the gentle giant, the large yet soft-spoken man who said very little unless it was important, jumped to his feet and growled, "Get the hell out of my house." Caught off guard and dumbfounded, the men asked him why he didn't want to march, but he shoved them out the door and said, "When you've seen what I've seen, you don't want to remember and you don't want to parade about it." Later on, it became clear that Grandpa was suffering from post-traumatic stress disorder, and once I realized this, so many things made sense.

Grandpa started to suffer from Alzheimer's disease towards the end of his life, and he eventually required the kind of care that can only be provided in a home. He would often wake up yelling, swearing, sometimes ending up crouched down beside his bed like it was a trench. Watching the fear and confusion in his eyes during those episodes was heartbreaking.

Grandpa Terrance died on January 28, 1994, at the age of ninety. Before his funeral, the scratched and dented lid of the old steamer trunk was lifted, and the medals were brought

into the light for the first time in a very long time, to be pinned to Grandpa's chest, which was a place I doubted they had been in fifty years, if at all. As his casket sat in the middle of the church, the Colour Party from the ANAVETS dipped their flags as the last post was played from a cassette. Looking back on it today, this was the moment when I decided to devote an immense chunk of my life to the study of military history,

The author's step-grandfather, Terrance Bear. Author's photo.

even going so far as to study it at Cambridge. To this day, I still go into elementary schools to teach young people about the sacrifices made by veterans for the freedoms that we enjoy, and to remind them that it cannot happen again.

In the summer of 2000, I found myself standing on Blackfriars Bridge in London, walking back to the Tube station that would take me to where I would catch the train back to Cambridge. I realized where I was, and a quick look at my watch let me know that it was nearly 10:00 a.m. I spun around, looking for the dome of St. Paul's Cathedral. I positioned myself facing across the bridge. I began to shuttle this way and that, trying to position myself in such a way that the dome was just in the corner of my eye. When I finally got myself into position, I could hear a church bell from somewhere way off behind me softly toll the hour of ten. I was standing, give or take a few feet this way or that, in roughly the same position Grandpa had stood some fifty years before me. I began to weep.

Perhaps it was premonition on his part that he chose to share his experiences with me. Of course, I am not under any illusions that I was the sole person he spoke with about them. In fact, I'm sure I'm not. They were extremely heavy tales and anecdotes to lay upon the mind and shoulders of an eleven-year-old boy, but they are tales that continue to live on in a way that provides the lesson to not take for granted what you have and who you have and what memories you have made in your life, for one day, they may be taken away.

When it comes to my biological grandfather, Jim Brady, I did not have the luxury of meeting him. His disappearance occurred when my mother was only fifteen years old, so any knowledge I have of him comes from the stories told by those whose lives he touched and the example he set.

I have always been deeply proud of the work of my grandfather, and I take every opportunity I get to share my pride and love for him, to the point where my phone's predictive text says, "Jim Brady is my grandfather."

Jim Brady is one of the most famous and highly regarded Métis leaders of the twentieth century. He was instrumental in the formation of the Métis Association of Alberta and the Métis Association of Saskatchewan, and he is forever held in the highest honour among the Métis for his contributions to the struggle for Métis rights and Métis identity.

To say that I take after him is beyond an understatement. Our physical appearance and facial features are remarkably similar, almost to the point of being twins or me being his doppelgänger. I have chosen to live my life every day emulating the principles, teachings and philosophies that he lived by: a humble, simple life free of materialism, with basic human decency towards others; a set of Marxist socialist ideals; and the continued fight for the rights of Indigenous and Métis people. I take every chance I can to keep his name and memory alive as one of the greatest leaders in Métis history. He is a man whom I never met, but his legacy has been my goalpost since the beginning.

I am blessed to come from a lineage of deep historical importance in Canadian history, particularly when it comes to Indigenous history.

My great-great-grandfather was Laurent Garneau. He was a Red River Métis, and he took part in the 1869 Rebellion

James Brady while serving in the
Second World War. Note the simi-
larity with his grandson, the author.
"James Brady, Metis, while in Holland." Courtesy of
the Glenbow Archives NA-3517-3.

John Brady McDonald.
Author's photo.

as one of Riel's soldiers. Later, he became a confidant of
him, and perhaps, as some say, a spy for Riel's council. My
great-great-grandfather would have watched the execution
of Thomas Scott, and he was there at the tumultuous birth
of the province of Manitoba.

It is at this point that two different branches of my
family tree possibly intersect. In the Red River Settlement,
Laurent would have likely crossed paths with another
man, an Orcadian Scot named James Dreaver, who had
journeyed to Canada to join the Hudson's Bay Company.
James Dreaver would soon venture west to the banks of
the North Saskatchewan River at Prince Albert, marry a
daughter of Chief Mistawasis and become my grandmother's
great-grandfather.

By 1874, Laurent Garneau had moved west and settled
with his wife, Eleanor, on land in what is now the city of

Edmonton, Alberta. In fact, the district where his original farm was located is still known today as Garneau, and he is seen as one of the founding leaders of the community.

During the 1885 Resistance, Laurent kept written correspondence with Riel. It seems likely that my great-great-grandfather was still serving as an informant to Riel, keeping him in the loop about what was occurring in the Edmonton area.

There is a family legend regarding how very close Laurent came to losing his freedom, and quite possibly his life, for his loyalty to Riel, but was saved by the quick work of his wife, Eleanor.

As the family legend goes, around the time of the second resistance of the Métis in 1885, Canadian soldiers burst into the home of Laurent and Eleanor. My great-great-grandfather was seized by the soldiers, and informed that his house was to be searched for any documentation linking him to Riel and to the resistance, and if found, my great-great-grandfather was to be hung. My great-great-grandmother sat calmly beside her washtub, vigorously scrubbing a pair of Laurent's trousers on her washboard. The house was searched, but no evidence was found, no letters, no documentation, so the soldiers departed.

They had no idea that, much like Edgar Allan Poe's "The Purloined Letter," the evidence they sought was in plain view the whole time.

You see, as the soldiers came through the door, Eleanor gathered the papers together and stuffed them into the pocket of one of Laurent's trousers, then proceeded to obliterate them against the washboard. As the soldiers tossed her

The family of Laurent and Eleanor Garneau. The author's great-grandmother is on the far right. "Garneau Family." City of Edmonton Archives EA-58-4.

house, she destroyed the evidence they sought right in front of them, and they were none the wiser.

At the turn of the century, Laurent and Eleanor, along with many of their children, left Edmonton and settled in the community of St.-Paul-des-Métis, after a land dispute. One of their daughters, Philomena Archange, became the first Métis registered nurse in Alberta. In time, she would marry an Irish immigrant, and, in 1908, she gave birth to a son. Laurent would pass on his knowledge and his ferocious fight for Métis rights to his grandson, Jim Brady. Laurent Garneau died in 1918.

My grandfather was born James Patrick Brady Jr. on April 11, 1908, near Lake St. Vincent, Alberta. He was a self-educated man, building a vast knowledge of history and politics that would lead him to be one of the greatest political minds in Métis history. He learned politics at the feet of his grandfather, and he became what was then known as a "worker intellectual" – an itinerant labourer who would travel from work site to logging camp, toiling all day and teaching others by night. My grandfather continued to solidify and codify his theories and knowledge into what became his life's work – the movement towards the betterment of the lives of the Métis of western Canada.

In the politically tumultuous days of the 1920s, Jim Brady was at the forefront of nearly every major political event that involved the Métis. He was part of what was known as "The Famous Five," a collection of Métis men (himself, Malcolm Norris, Peter Tomkins, Joe Dion and Felix Callihoo) who organized the various factions among the Métis peoples of Alberta into what is now the Métis Nation of Alberta.

As a result of their efforts, these men took part in the Ewing Commission, which heard testimony and took evidence speaking to the degradation, deprivation and abuses suffered by the Métis of Alberta, which in turn lead to the passage of the 1938 Métis Population Betterment Act.

The Big Five. Back Row, left to right: Peter Tompkins and Felix Calliou. Front Row: Malcolm Norris, Joseph Dion and Jim Brady. "Group portrait of the Provincial Executive Committee, Alberta Metis Association." Courtesy of the Glenbow Archives PA-2218-109.

Jim Brady was a lifelong Marxist socialist, as well as a member of the Communist Party of Canada. It was these political affiliations that, in 1941, lead to the Canadian Army refusing to enlist him during the Second World War. It is preposterous to think that during a time when the world's armies were calling out for able-bodied men to enlist, here was a man who had to fight to be allowed to fight. He was denied

James Brady with his daughter Emma, the mother of the author, 1961.
"James Brady and Emma Jean Bird." Courtesy of the Glenbow Archives PA-2218-931.

enlistment until 1943, when he became a gunner with the Royal Canadian Artillery, seeing action in France, Belgium and the Netherlands.

After the war, he returned to Saskatchewan, where, in 1952, he fathered my mother, whom he loved very much. Many books glance over and overlook the relationship that he had with my mother and my grandmother, often times focusing in on the children he had while living in Cumberland House, Saskatchewan. My mother is often described as being born several years earlier in Cumberland House – a place she has never actually been. Many times, his relationship with my grandmother and my mother is made to seem insignificant and meaningless, or worse, that there was a sense of shame or disconnect between them all. Yet, if you read the hand-written letters he sent to my mother, or you listen to the eyewitness testimony of those who were there, it becomes obvious that this was a man who deeply cared for and loved both my grandmother and my mother, and ensured that they were looked after and cared for until his disappearance. In her last years, though she was happily married to the man I grew up knowing and loving as my grandpa, and who had been her partner for the better part of forty years, whenever my grandmother spoke of Jim Brady you could still see the affection and care for him in her eyes.

Jim Brady made his home in La Ronge, Saskatchewan. He lived in a small cabin he built on a rock off a main road. This was his home when he disappeared in June 1967. There is a wonderful book called *Cold Case North*, by Michael Nest, Deanna Reder and Eric Bell, which is an amazingly deep look into the circumstances of his disappearance and the recent expeditions and discoveries as Reder, Bell and others continue to search for his remains. I will not attempt to cover the same ground here.

My grandfather's cabin was known as a place where a hungry stomach, a frozen body or an inquisitive mind was never turned away. I had heard about this cabin my whole life from my mother, of how the attic was stuffed with books and how my grandfather held socialist and Marxist conversations for hours on end. In the latter half of the 1990s and 2000s, however, it had fallen into disrepair and become a drinking place.

In the summer of 2001, I found myself in La Ronge for the Saskatchewan Aboriginal Summer Games. I wanted to finally visit this place, where the fire of my socialist activism was lit before I was even born. I have no physical belongings from

Jim Brady in front of his cabin in La Ronge, Saskatchewan. McDonald family collection.

The author standing in the same position as his grandfather in front of his grandfather's cabin in La Ronge, Saskatchewan, Summer 2001. Author's photo.

my grandfather, no tangible ephemera or object he held in his hands. I only have my strong physical resemblance and other people's memories of him. I wanted to go to the place where he once lived, in order to be as close to him as possible.

The house stood on a rock outcropping back in the bush behind a credit union, accessible by an overgrown path littered with empty liquor and Listerine bottles, scraps of clothing, the wrappers from syringes and other piles of garbage. The detritus of substance abuse and poverty.

The shack was painted with peeling white paint and peeling black trim. It was situated on a north-south axis, with its front facing south. The door of the structure was gone, and the inside was an open, filthy space that smelled of years of urine, vomit and excrement. The debris inside showed plainly the building's use as a place where the homeless and addicted of La Ronge congregated to drink, to get high, to shit and piss and keep out of the eye of the public and law enforcement. There was nothing left that reflected the tales that my mother told me of her time there – the partition wall between the living area and a small bedroom area; the loft that was crammed with what was at one time the largest private library in Saskatchewan, some 4,500 titles; the typewriter that she remembered playing on; or even the window she remembered looking out. It had been boarded over.

In front of the cabin and to the left, there was what appeared to be a small cement cairn, chipped and worn, which appeared to have, at one time, held a plaque, long since gone.

There is a photo of my grandfather standing in front of his home, a cigarette in his hand. It is also on the back cover of the book *The One-and-a-Half Men* by Murray Dobbin.

I knew that I had to recreate this photo, to stand where he stood, and while I have the smoke in the wrong hand, it is a photo that I am so very happy to have. I was a much younger, thinner man than I am now, and I only had the slightest inkling how much my life was about to change within a few short years. I also snapped a photo of my girlfriend in front of the cabin. In time, we married and, as you read this, we still are.

My photos could be the only known colour photos of this cabin, I do not know. The building, after years of abuse and becoming both an eyesore and a hazard, was finally donated by my aunt to the local fire department for use as a live fire training exercise, which, as a former firefighter

myself, I appreciated and understood. I managed to track
down photos from the La Ronge Regional Fire Department
of what was apparently that live fire exercise. I have visited
the site once more since then. The poplar trees and under-
brush are beginning to take over the site, yet the footprint
of the cabin upon its rock outcropping is still visible beneath
the tall grasses and litter.

I am purposely choosing to close this piece on the
discussion of photographs for a very important reason, as
photographs have played such an import role in my explo-
ration of my grandfather and his life. Indeed, it has been
through archival photographs that I have been able to see
not only my great great-grandparents and their children,
but also, for the first time, James Patrick Brady Sr., my
great-grandfather, and to know what he looked like. As of
this writing, there is a photographic exhibit of my grandfather's photos, curated by Paul Seesequasis, on display
in the Glenbow Museum in Calgary, the repository of my
grandfather's archives. My grandfather is believed by Paul
Seesequasis to be the first Indigenous photographer of merit.

For my entire life, my grandfather existed to me only in
black-and-white photographs. I had spent decades trying to
discover a colour photograph of him, to no avail. I had seen
a colourized version of the well-known 1935 photograph of
the "Famous Five," which showed him as a younger man,
but no matter how well done, colourized photos fail to truly
capture what colour film will.

In February of 2020, as we all began to hunker down for
what was to become the COVID pandemic, I was scrolling

This is the only known colour photograph of Jim Brady, taken in La Ronge, Saskatchewan, on July 1, 1966, less than a year before he disappeared. He is behind the bagpiper. © Don Neely, courtesy of Craig Neely.

through social media, when, out of the blue, a photo came up on a page dedicated to the visual history of La Ronge, Saskatchewan.

It was an image of the July 1, 1966, Canada Day parade in La Ronge, taken by a man named Don Neely. The photo was posted by his son, Craig Neely, who was going through his father's photos and sharing any of interest regarding La Ronge.

I have been a keen follower of this online group, scrutinizing every single period photograph posted for a glimpse of my grandfather, but, surprisingly, I had missed this one.

The photograph shows a lone bagpiper in a kilt preceding a row of older men marching in dark suits and berets. While there are no insignia or Royal Canadian Legion badges visible, it is safe to assume, due to formation and berets, that these are veterans.

At the front of this row of veterans, his head forward and his eyes looking down, was a face I knew beyond well, as it is the same face that I see in the mirror every morning. It was my grandfather. For the first time, I could see the true colour of his complexion, the way the light hit his face and the posture he held as he moved, so similar to my own. I began to weep, and every now and then, I look at it and still do.

July 1, 2020

Your Canada is 153 years old.

My ancestral connection to the land, shackled by Your Canada, goes back far beyond your concept of time. The land upon which you celebrate is where my ancestors buried their ancestors.

For you, it's the celebration of lines drawn on a map, a construct of cartography.

For me, I connect with my blood when I touch the soil with my bare hands. My DNA doesn't lie in that soil. It IS that soil, for there are generations of human beings who have passed over this land, and have had their bodies decay and return to this land, their bodies forever part of the earth, their atomic particles disentangling themselves from the shapes of arms and legs and torsos and becoming one with the deep brown soil, becoming nutrients within it.

Do I observe the day? No, not in that way. It is not celebrating, but mourning and remembering old teachings that I do.

Carrying It Forward

We are surrounded in Your Canada, Your United States and Your Americas by great multitudes of lost teachings. Stone circles and sophisticated cave dwellings and massive images scratched onto the surface of the earth and visible only from space, but to name a few. You know these sites, for they are often said to have been created by visitors from other worlds, for my ancestors were considered far too primitive by European standards to have the ability to create such things, yet they are here. They exist, created by Indigenous hands.

The scholars look at and speculate about these places, these marks on the walls, these clay pots and these sacred sites, wondering their purpose.

What would you do if you found out?

I was taught that when a teaching is lost, it is not our responsibility as Knowledge Carriers to simply mourn and lament the loss. It is our duty to also take what we can learn from what is left and reinterpret what it means to us now, to be resilient and, if need be, forge a new lesson from a lost one.

We are sadly so far removed from many of our traditional teachings. Too many of our pre-contact ways are lost forever.

Thus, we as Indigenous people here in Your Canada, Your Americas, must do what we have always done. We must fall upon our resiliency and forge ahead. In order for the Red Road to survive, I personally believe that we can no longer look at lost teachings, rock art or stone circles and simply say, "This teaching is lost." I feel that it is our responsibility to look at these sacred things and say, "What does this mean to me now?" I feel that it is our responsibility to create new teachings. We are the future ancestors.

I am sitting out in the bush as I write this, a pen and paper in my hand. The leaves of the poplar trees rattle in the canopy above me, as they have done for more years than Your Canada can imagine, and my thoughts are with so many members of my circle who have suffered such tragic losses over the past few days.

I always bring tobacco out to the bush with me, and provide offerings for a safe return home. If I am hunting, I am thanking and honouring the spirit of the animal for giving its life to feed my family, and remembering those who have taught me so much about *Nêhiyawâtisiw*, living the Cree way, with the earth.

I also leave tobacco for those whose hearts are broken. My social media is often overwhelmed with close friends or acquaintances who have lost family members, and I often acknowledge these losses with "Tobacco Down for your loss."

I've been asked why, when someone has lost a loved one, I respond with "Tobacco Down." When I say this, it is not merely an empty gesture or meaningless phrase like "thoughts and prayers." When I say "Tobacco Down," I actually go out into the bush and make an offering of tobacco to a particular tree, made sacred by the intent I place upon it. This is a way of honouring that person's *waskochepayis*, that one hundred watts of electrical energy that exists in the nervous systems of all human beings, which keeps our hearts beating and our lungs breathing. When we die, that electrical energy returns somewhere, back into the eternal power grid of life on earth, and that electricity is sacred.

I have stated many times that I do not worship in a religious way any form of Creator or omnipotent being. It is my way. I seek tangible scientific proof, and that is provided when it comes to *waskochepayis*. It is scientifically measurable. This is the life force I honour when I put tobacco down, and when I say it, I mean it. This is but one way to adapt old teachings in Your Canada, and it is not a new concept.

When I smudge, I use matches to light the sage. When I dance powwow, the music is amplified using a microphone. When I am gifted tobacco for my teachings, it is from a store.

We have adapted fairly well in Your Canada. It's what we do best.

My Regalia

My regalia is old. It is not the fancy, flashy regalia of today. My regalia is made from what I have gathered over twenty-five years. It is made of white and black scraps of cloth, without beads or sequins. The scraps of cloth came from a bag of material I found tucked in the back of a storage room at a youth centre where I worked for many years.

I wear a plastic beaded breastplate I made when I was an eighteen-year-old student and beginning my return to the Red Road. The beads came from a pile of discarded projects left behind and unfinished by other students – dream catchers and chokers and key chains – and I had to meticulously undo someone else's abandoned work to create one of my own. The effort and energy that they partially put into their work goes with me as I dance.

My fringes are but ribbons from a bag of athletic medals I got at a second-hand store, all strips of red, white and blue ribbons, sewn as a fringe from my breechclout and gauntlets, chosen to represent my journeys into the United States, the United Kingdom and Australia – the national flags of those colours – land upon which I had partaken in ceremony. Underneath it all, I wear a pair of old black sweatpants and a dress shirt, a nod to my rebellious youth, my tribute to Johnny Cash and the metalhead I was then and still am.

I have no bustle or moccasins. My headdress is made from crow, goose and hawk feathers, zip-tied and held to an old ball cap with sinew and electrical tape. The hawk feathers came from a bird I saw hit by a vehicle in front of me on a dusty rural back road one summer. I stopped and picked up the bird, and it died in my hands. I felt its life force dissipate, and I honoured the bird by making sure that its feathers would feel the wind again.

My shield looks like overcooked and dried-out bannock. The moose hide shield was a gift from a young offender whom I once counselled on the outside. Though the shield is small and misshapen, darkened and warped, he took great pride in its creation, and, for the first time, followed the proper channels to make sure I got it.

The choker I wear around my neck was made by a young lady in foster care, who made it for me as a gift for reasons known only to herself. She was in a group home, and, shortly after she made the choker for me, she left the group home, and I have not seen her since.

The only decoration I have on any of it is a single black handprint. This design was given to me by a Lakota Elder many years ago in the Black Hills of South Dakota. The handprint is a powerful symbol, and the teachings and reasons I was gifted it as my mark will forever remain between me and that Elder. While my role is to educate and to teach, there will forever be things that will remain private and secret. There are many teachings and ceremonies that are not for public consumption. They are sacred rites and teachings held in private reserve for those following the traditional ways of their people. They are held sacred and private for many reasons.

Remember that, for decades, many traditional practices, teachings and ceremonies were outlawed across much of North America, and the residential schools tried their best to beat the culture out of us. Our traditional and spiritual ways have been under attack since the first Christian Cross was brought ashore centuries ago, and it is completely understandable that some of our teachings are not meant to be shared with others. They watched and heard the stories of sacred big drums, eagle feathers, medicine bundles and sweat lodges being burned in bonfires. They had their mouths slapped when speaking their language. They were eyewitnesses to the destruction. Our Elders and ancestors took our ways underground, hid them, protected them against destruction. Sacred songs were sung while keeping the beat with the bass drum from a marching band or drum kit, regalia made from rags, yarn, flour sacks and what have you. The ways continued in spite of the destruction, and part of that was due to the fact that they were protective of them.

Compared to the other powwow dancers, I look ragged and poor, which is true on both counts, and I'm never going to win any competitions or prizes.

That's not why I dance, however. I dance to heal, and to connect with who I am as an Indigenous warrior. I dance because the Big Drum speaks to me.

The ways in which we express ourselves in our culture, be it through dance, through singing, through visual art, through teaching, however one chooses to express themselves, those ways are all *maskihkiy*, they are medicine. It is how we heal, and the actions and the intent of the person teaching, the practitioner of the medicine, often dictate the lesson we learn from the medicine.

The first time that I ever sat down at the Big Drum was in grade ten. I was invited by Victor Thunderchild, my high school Cree teacher. This was the teacher who first helped me set my steps onto the Red Road. He was the first to welcome me to the Big Drum, to offer me a drumstick and to add my beat to the song. I was a scrawny, scruffy teenager from the bad side of town, with long messy hair, a black leather jacket and a bad attitude, and Victor gave me the chance to reconnect with that part of me.

On April 17, 2021, Victor Thunderchild tragically lost his life as a result of COVID-19. He was only fifty-five years old. His death, the first death of a teacher in the province of Saskatchewan as a result of COVID-19, absolutely gutted and devastated the community. To say that he was a beloved teacher would be an understatement. Victor touched so many lives, and he was truly loved by those of us who knew him, who learned from him, who shared the drum with him and who crossed his path.

When I was a student at the Won-Ska Cultural School, I was honoured to sing alongside my fellow students. I was always the lightest-skinned singer at the drum, but I was never made to feel that I did not belong at the drum, and I knew that I was part of this cultural heritage and way of life that dates far back into the past. I remember the first time the lead singer gestured towards me across the drum, telling me in that unspoken way, "Okay, it's your turn to sing lead on this one." I was so nervous, but I think I did okay.

In time, I was given the honour of being a drumkeeper, given a few songs and told to share them with the young people.

When I was a younger artist, I painted a lot of stereotypical "Indigenous" paintings: eagles and tipis and buffalo skulls and the like. Whenever I saw tipis, be it at a powwow or any other gathering, I always noticed a long red ribbon flying from one of the poles. As such, whenever I painted a tipi, I dutifully painted a long red ribbon flying from one of the poles.

I always wondered about the symbolism of that long red ribbon. I never knew what spiritual or ceremonial meanings it held. I never questioned it, though I wanted to know very badly.

I finally decided to discover, after so many years, what that ribbon meant. At a ceremony, I approached an Elder. I presented him with tobacco. "*Mohsom*," I asked, "what is the meaning of that red ribbon on the tipi?"

He accepted my tobacco, and he nodded in all seriousness as only a wise person can when queried. "My boy," he said, "that is actually a teaching that comes from our white brothers. That is one of their teachings."

I was astonished. "What does it mean?" I asked.

He closed his eyes and nodded again. "My boy, our white brothers have taught us... if you have anything hanging more than six feet off the back of a vehicle, you have to tie a red flag on it."

This is Indigenous *ka waninehk*, the humour for which Indigenous people are known. It is nuanced and structured in such a way that it is difficult to explain to someone outside of the circle.

Not all teachings are positive. I remember when my world view began to change for me away from a belief in a Creator. It was at a gathering of Elders and Knowledge Keepers along the shores of Manitou Lake, Saskatchewan. I was asked to keep a fire for a sweat for a group of cultural advisors and Elders who work in the correctional system. In Cree, the helper of an Elder at ceremonies is called *oskâpêwis*. This was the first time I had kept the fire for this particular group of individuals.

As the sweat was moving to its final round, I had gathered the remaining stones together in a pile in the fire, and had them resting on the tines of a pitchfork, ready to go in as soon as they were called for, as I had been shown to do by the Elders for whom I had kept the fire before. The door of the sweat opened, and one of the men poked his head out, saw this and yelled at me loudly to "GET THOSE STONES OFF THAT FORK!!!" He jumped out of the sweat and snatched the fork away from me. He made me feel about an inch tall. I walked away from the lodge.

He later approached me with tobacco, and tried to explain why he yelled, but at no point did he apologize. He went on to mention that if the Creator had wanted those stones to be on that fork, then the Creator would have put them there. When he finished his spiel, I looked at him, handed his tobacco back, gestured towards the lodge and said, "You have ruined this for me forever, because any time I will ever go near a lodge, all I will hear is you." It has been almost ten years. I have not kept fire for a sweat since. It was a harsh reminder of the humanity of those who are often held in high esteem. I hope that I will one day be able to sit in the lodge, to keep fire once again, and not see that man or hear his words, but it may be a long time before this wound heals.

When the medicine is good, it speaks to people. I've watched as, in front of a gymnasium full of people, a shy young boy jumped out of the audience, sat down at the drum without an invitation and began to drum with us. It spoke to him in a way that he needed to hear at that moment, much like it did for me so very long ago. It is medicine of the most-high, it is our heartbeat, and I am humbled and honoured to share it.

While a proper bustle and some moccasins would be nice, I don't think I'd want a "nice" outfit. My regalia represents the scavenger survivor spirit I carry as a warrior as well as the resiliency that has kept me going this entire time. It represents who I am, and where I came from. I wear these stories upon my heart and upon my body for those who have, as Hunter S. Thompson once said, "the right kind of eyes."

Postscript: May 2021

As I write this, I have begun to create a bustle for my regalia.

The forty-eight long, black feathers, pulled one at a time from the wings of geese taken by a Métis hunter and gifted to me, lay spread out across the kitchen table in two parallel curves, twenty-four feathers to a side, matched up as evenly and similarly as possible with its match on the other side.

The feathers have sat in my basement for just over a year. I had gathered them in the autumn prior to the start of the pandemic, with plans to begin work the next spring. Sadly, that was the spring that COVID-19 spread across the globe, and any thoughts of creating anything were put aside in the chaos and stress that such a tragedy spews forth.

It is admittedly odd that, shortly after receiving the first of my COVID-19 vaccinations, the desire to create once again began to grow inside me. I found my thoughts turning to the half-finished project in my studio, and when I began to work on it, there was not the inclination to put it down and leave it. A friend described it as "the first taste of Peace of Mind in forever." While I'm pretty sure that it will be a very long time, if ever again, before we return to a naive state of full Peace of Mind, I would be inclined to entertain the thought that, yes, it is but the lifting of the foot for the first step of a return to a normalized existence.

The bustle will continue to follow the scavenger–urban

Indigenous story that the rest of my regalia tells. The feathers, somewhat rough from their fall from the sky, are mounted together with loops of plastic zip ties, secured to the shafts of each feather with strips of black and red electrical tape. The black and red strips are to honour my late uncle Fred Sasakamoose, who was the first Indigenous person with Treaty Status to play in the NHL. He played eleven games with the Chicago Black Hawks in 1955 before returning home to Saskatchewan. Uncle Fred died in November of 2020 at the age of eighty-six as a result of COVID-19. As the Chicago colours are black and red, I will carry Uncle Fred into the powwow circle in my own way. They will probably be mounted to an old compact disc, which will hopefully be able to support the weight of it all. If not, then they will be mounted to a small piece of plywood, painted black.

As each feather is readied for the final assembly of the bustle, I find my thoughts going back to the time when I was invited to dance powwow in Sydney, New South Wales, Australia, in April of 2001, at the request of a youth organization who had heard me speak at a conference in South Dakota. I remember the intense tropical heat causing the hair of the coyote headdress I wore to stick to my face, the sweat pouring down and soaking my borrowed regalia. When I had finished the dance, the Indigenous Australian Elder who had delivered the opening prayer came over and embraced me, calling me "Little Brother."

I hope that by the time the bustle is complete, we will be able to gather once again in the arbour and dance together to the Big Drum under open skies. Only time and human nature will tell. Until then, I continue to wrap each feather, one at a time, visiting rooms in my memory palace that have gone unvisited for far too long.

The Flag Thing

In the Canadian Museum of History in Ottawa, on the Gatineau side of the river, along a curved wall in what is known as the First Peoples Hall, there is a collection of artifacts pertaining to the history of First Nations, Métis and Inuit peoples in Canada.

As of this writing, the museum is currently closed to visitors, so what I am about to describe may or may not be accurate any longer.

In one portion of the First Peoples Hall rests a collection of items. There is a Calgary Flames jersey, worn by Akina Shirt when she became the first person in Canadian history to sing the national anthem in an Indigenous language at a major sporting event, when she sang "O Canada" in Cree on February 3, 2007, before a Calgary Flames–Vancouver Canucks game. There is a Métis buckskin jacket, said to have belonged to Louis Riel, in a glass display case, as well as a wooden cradleboard and a piece of Inuit art presumably by famed artist Kenojuak Ashevak. Hanging from the ceiling at an angle is a full-sized birchbark canoe.

Above it all is a flag.

The flag is three feet by five feet, and the creases are still visible from nearly twenty years of being folded away. It appears to be a standard Canadian flag. However, over the maple leaf is the image of an Indigenous man in buckskin, with eight or so large feathers in his long hair, a braid to his right and a ceremonial pipe in his left hand as he gazes stoically to his left.

This flag has been called many things – the Canada Indian Flag, the Canada Native American Flag, the Canada Indian Chief Flag and so on. For the purposes of clarity, I will call it the Canadian Indigenous Warrior Flag. It comes in many variations of colour and quality. The complexion of the man varies from white and yellow to a very dark shade of brown. Sometimes, the top three points of the maple leaf protrude over his head, and sometimes they don't. Sometimes the detail in his face and clothing is well-defined, and other times it is shoddy and blurry. There are variations of the flag where the warrior is on an American flag, or, oddly, a Confederate battle flag.

The true name and history of the flag is murky. It first appeared sometime in the 1980s, and it became a well-known and ubiquitous symbol in "NDN Country." It became a symbol of Indigenous resistance to Canadian colonialism, and a reminder that Canada and the Indigenous people are often still at odds with one another.

While it is a somewhat rare find today, there was a time when this flag could be found for sale in many novelty shops, offered by fairground vendors and sold at powwows. It could be found hanging on walls or over windows as a curtain in many Indigenous homes both on and off reserve. For a moment in Indigenous history, it was everywhere.

I can tell you very specifically, however, about the journey of the particular flag in question, and how it came to be hanging on display in Ottawa. This flag played a significant role in an event that changed my life in ways that cannot be described, though I shall try my best. This is the first time that I have ever provided a definitive, written account of the event, so please bear with me.

The flag the author used to symbolically "claim" England, on display in the First Peoples Hall, Canadian Museum of History, Gatineau, Quebec.
Author's photo.

In June of 1999, four students of the Won-Ska Cultural School in Prince Albert, Saskatchewan, were invited to the Black Hills of South Dakota, to speak at a series of seminars regarding youth that were, at that time, still referred to as "at-risk" kids. I was one of those students.

The seminars were sponsored by advocates of a wonderfully successful philosophy of working with children with behavioural and emotional issues called the Circle of Courage, based upon traditional Lakota teachings. The Circle of Courage provides a troubled young person with a positive sense of belonging (as opposed to the sense of belonging they might find with a gang), a sense of mastery and self-control within themselves, a sense of independence from addiction, criminality and so forth and teaches them to set their own goals, all with the hope that they will one day gain a sense of generosity, passing what they've learned on to others.

Won-Ska based its operation and existence around this same philosophy. The name of the school was derived from the Nêhiyawak word *waniska*, meaning "to wake up," and for many years it had been successfully serving as an Indigenous culture–based option for Indigenous students who, for various reasons, either could not be successful in a regular high school setting or had dropped out and were trying to reconnect with their culture while at the same time achieving a high school education. The four of us were asked to go down to the United States to share our stories, and to share what this philosophy had done for us.

I think about Won-Ska often. I remember its wide hallways and doorways, the perpetual scent of burnt sage and sweetgrass in the air, the soft murmur of the students in the classrooms, the ring of the telephone, the occasional sound of powwow music and the warmth of the air stepping into the building for the first time.

I dream about it at least once a week, such is the impact upon my life made by that place. In the dreams, I walk into classrooms and past open doorways, searching for familiar faces or familiar scenes, but feeling an overwhelming sense of frustration at the changes and modifications my sleeping brain is making, altering an already injured series of memories even further.

Perhaps it's because I have never really had the chance to properly mourn the loss of it, not solely the loss caused by moving on as my academic studies took me farther away and I left the nest, as it were, but to honestly grieve the loss of a place as I once knew it. Is it silly for one to mourn the ever-evolving dynamics of an institution? Perhaps it is made harder still as I was there when the keys to the ignition were handed over, and I felt as if I was the last remaining vestige of what the school had been. I felt my eternal urge to speak for those who were no longer there to speak for themselves and then I felt helpless as I watched the tail lights turn the corner and drive out of sight.

I was seventeen when I first walked through those doors to Won-Ska. I had officially been a high school dropout for an entire school year, drifting aimlessly, trying whatever I could and however I could to numb and silence the pain I was experiencing at that point in my life. My circle of acquaintances, the choices I was making and the lifestyle in which I found myself entrenched were leading me into a dangerous and dark place. At the time, I had no idea that I was trying to cover the pain of years of trauma I had suffered as a child. I was a teenager, and I was doing what I thought teenagers did.

My regular high school career ended with an escort out of the building and a ban from the premises for life by the red-faced old man whose desk I had flipped and whose mother I had invited him to go and fuck after making the almighty sin of asking for help. I had been met with the response "Why should I bother helping you? You're just going to end up either dead or in jail, just like the rest of them." Several things were smashed, and phone calls made to the police, no doubt, but my days as a student at that particular institution had come to an end. I walked the hour from the school to where I was staying with my leather biker jacket wrapped tightly around me to combat a February in Saskatchewan; my only concern was what I was going to use to numb this pain as well.

Many months later, I found myself in the home of a respected Elder. I sat at his table eating a meal. He looked at me, and he asked, "My boy, why aren't you in school?"

I chose my words very carefully, not wanting to upset him. "I just couldn't work there, *Mohsom*," I said, referring to him by the Nêhiyawak word for *grandfather*. In our language, we refer to all older relatives as either aunts and uncles, or, if they are much older, grandmothers and grandfathers. The kinship dynamic of Indigenous culture is such that we are always in a constant search for familial connections, and even when that connection is tenuous at best, that individual is considered to be and accepted into your circle as family. The deep appreciation of kinship is one of the most beautiful aspects of Indigenous culture. One is never without someone who will fill the role of auntie, cousin or *kohkom*.

The old man looked at me, then at his cup of tea. He thought for a long while before he spoke. This is another beautiful trait among our people. When the Elders speak, they will say something...then there will be a very long, very pregnant pause before they say something else...then another pause, and so on. This is not simply a deliberate choice upon the speaker. That individual is weighing carefully every single word they are about to say, and they are thinking about the consequences and outcomes of their words, for once the words leave their mouths, they are responsible for any emotions, actions or reactions that come about as a result. They take responsibility for anything that happens as a result of what they have said. It has always been this way; well-chosen and crafted words spoken with the utmost care and consideration.

When he finally did speak, he said, "Tomorrow, you're going to come with me."

The next morning, bright and early, the old man's car pulled up to a flat, squat building that sat on an east-west access at the bottom of a hill, beneath the abandoned building that once housed the Catholic elementary school I attended for a few weeks in kindergarten, and farther still from the ancient Edwardian public school where I had briefly spent a few months in grade three and four on either side of a summer during my transient early education.

The building was beige-brown and a long concrete wheel-chair ramp led up to the wide front doors. Along the side of the building, above a row of windows, on a sign flanked by Indigenous art, were yellow, hand-painted letters upon a blue-and-black backdrop depicting spruce trees. The letters read WON-SKA CULTURAL SCHOOL.

At one time, this building had been known as the "Kinsmen School," and it had been a school for students who were physically and intellectually challenged. I had a vague memory about being in this building as a small child, as a student, perhaps, on a classroom outing or field trip. I have a vague memory of sitting in ski pants and my winter coat on the floor as a presentation was being made. It must have been a very early memory, for the edges of it are fuzzy and threadbare, but as we pulled up to the curb that day that memory came back to me and I was not sure how to process it.

I opened the doors and stepped into the building. As I did, the scent of burning sage entered my nostrils for the first time.

I immediately felt my knees go weak beneath me, and I found myself suddenly unable to move forward. It was as if a switch had flipped somewhere deep inside me; some unknown, ancient inherent memory that the residential school had not managed to find and destroy. I felt the tears come to my eyes, and I felt the corners of my mouth turn down, as they do when I am about to have a deep, emotional bawl.

That day changed the trajectory of my life forever. I knew that I was supposed to be there. I knew that I was in a safe place, a welcoming place, warm and secure, and I knew that I had found a place to belong. That day nearly a quarter of a century ago is what gave me a second chance and I took it and ran with it.

One year later I found myself in South Dakota. It was my first time speaking about my life and my experiences in front of anyone, let alone five hundred complete strangers from around the world while in a foreign country one thousand kilometres from home. I was incredibly nervous, I was emotional and I was extremely vulnerable, but nevertheless I shared my story.

Six months later, I was back at school in Saskatchewan. It was a bitterly cold winter that year, and the world was in the grips of the whole looming Y2K disaster fear.

I was sitting in class when the principal of the school, a man named Ron Bentley, who had been the one to take us to South Dakota, came into the classroom. "John, you have a phone call," he said.

I walked into his office, and picked up the receiver. "Hello?"

The voice on the other end of the line was Dr. Martin Brokenleg, one of the three minds, along with Dr. Larry Brendtro and Dr. Steve Van Bockern, behind the Circle of Courage philosophy. Martin is from the Rosebud Reservation in South Dakota, and it was he who brought the traditional Lakota teachings that helped create the Circle of Courage.

"Good afternoon, John! I just wanted to thank you once again for coming down to the Black Hills and sharing your story with us. I also wanted to let you know that, because we were so touched and moved by your story, and because of the strong academics you have shown, we would like to offer you the opportunity to attend university next summer!"

I was speechless. I did not know what to say, other than, "Uh, th-thank you!"

Martin wasn't finished. "Now, it's for the summer, and you will have to do an immense amount of studying and reading beforehand, do you understand?"

I was still in a daze. "I understand," I replied. My knees were going to rubber. I was an eighteen-year-old street kid, only about a year clean and sober, still trying to finish high school, and these relative strangers were offering me a chance to make my world a little bit better.

That's when I barely heard Martin say, "...and you're also going to need to get a passport and plane ticket."

Without thinking, I blurted out, "Passport? Where the hell are you sending me, man?"

There was a pause. "Have you ever heard of the University of Cambridge?"

I needed to sit down. Yes, I had heard of the University of Cambridge, one of the most academically prestigious universities on the planet, the place where the theory of gravity, the theory of evolution, DNA and so many other amazing discoveries were made. This was where the royal family were educated, where Stephen Hawking, Sir Isaac Newton and Charles Darwin were educated and taught. "Yes," I said, almost in a whisper.

"You have been awarded a scholarship to the University of Cambridge International History Summer School. Congratulations, young man."

I was stunned, and, when the phone call was over, I felt as if I was floating. I was exhilarated. I was euphoric. I was going to move to and study in England, even if it was for only a short time.

That unbridled euphoria lasted the walk from the principal's office back to the classroom. As I sat back down to my books, and the principal told the class the news, a fellow student leaned over and said, "You know, they probably only gave that to you because you look white, eh?"

It was a slap to the face that I was not expecting. As a light-skinned Indigenous person, I have had to fight for years to be recognized as Indigenous. I had managed to begin to turn my life around, and at the very moment I had someone not only recognize it, but reward my efforts, someone saw it as only a recognition of my pale skin. The flicker of self-doubt sparked, caught flame, but extinguished quickly. It was at that moment, I made the decision that I was going to make this a success, and I was not going to let down those who were willing to take a chance on a skinny little street kid.

Thus began six months of extensive prerequisite studying, reading and examination. I took all of the books I was required to read over to the local bus station and put them on a scale. It weighed over one hundred pounds. I had to familiarize myself with rudimentary Greek (I studied both Greek political rhetoric and the literary representation of war in modern society), and, on top of that, mentally prepare to be a nineteen-year-old kid on his own on the other side of the Atlantic. It was an intense half-year of preparation, but I persevered as best as I could.

After Martin Brokenleg mentioned that I needed a passport, I was told by others that I would have to travel to the Government of Canada offices in Saskatoon to get it quicker than if I mailed away for it. This is what had me in Ron Bentley's vehicle headed to Saskatoon in February of 2000, just after my birthday.

"So," Ron said after a few kilometres of silence. "How are you feeling about going to the land of the Colonizers?"

I was puzzled. At this time, the words *colonization* and *settler* were not part of the common vernacular, as they are in today's society. I asked him to clarify.

"Well," he continued. "You're flying over to the land of the people who took your land and claimed it for themselves."

I chuckled, "Yeah, it'd be funny if…"

"If you went over there and did the same thing?"

A few more awkward moments of silence. "Yeah," I replied. "It would be funny, wouldn't it?"

By the time we reached Saskatoon the plan was in place.

The tales of European explorers and colonizers arriving in North America, then claiming large portions of the land for the various crowned heads of Europe has been taught in relatively the same fashion for too many years. These guys "discovered" the "New World." This narrative, built upon the exploits of Christopher Columbus, Jacques Cartier, John Cabot, Samuel de Champlain, Hernán Cortés and many others, pretends that this land was largely uninhabited and free for the taking, completely disregarding the millions of Indigenous people who had thriving and flourishing civilizations across the Americas and who have been here for tens of thousands of years. When the public narrative did finally change, it simply shifted "first to discover" away from Columbus and gave it to the Norse. If we were mentioned at all, it was as primitive savage aggressors, a violent and constant threat to these brave and intrepid explorers to this New Land. More recently, the attempt to change the narrative to a more palatable one has seen Indigenous people – often referred to in a bizarre phrasing of ownership as "our Indigenous people" – supposedly welcoming these travellers in the spirit of admiration and friendship. This ignores the slaughter and rape of entire nations at the hands of Columbus and the Spanish, and the genocidal decimation at the hands of the imperial English and French through disease and alcohol as they pushed ever westward in the pursuit of Manifest Destiny.

As I was an Indigenous student, travelling to a land where I had never been, a land with a civilization going back centuries, this was a perfect opportunity to "put the moccasin on the other foot," as it were. I was going to symbolically "discover" and "claim" England for the First Peoples of the Americas. I was going to plant a flag, right there, in front of Buckingham Palace, and I knew just which flag I was going to use.

The Canadian Indigenous Warrior Flag had gone into battle many times. It flew over most of the protests and acts of Indigenous resistance in the 1980s and 1990s. When that flag was flown over a roadblock or during a demonstration, it showed that there were Indigenous warriors there. It was a symbol of, to use period-correct terminology, "Native Resistance."

In April 2000, I walked into Tramp's Music and Books on Central Avenue in Prince Albert. This was, and still is (though now in a different location), Prince Albert's comic book store, and the place to buy rock T-shirts, trading cards, CDs, posters and used books. It also sold flags, including the Canadian Indigenous Warrior Flag. I purchased one for approximately ten dollars.

The flag flew to England with me in my carry-on luggage, which turned out to be a wise decision, as the remainder of my luggage spent two weeks lost somewhere between Calgary International Airport and Heathrow Airport in London.

When I stepped off the plane that rainy July morning in London, I could not anticipate the level to which my entire world would be changed forever. I remember a quote from a historian regarding Indigenous veterans returning from the Second World War and how they were expected to go back to being "good little Indians" in their home communities after fighting in Europe. The historian said, "How can a man be expected to simply go back to the Rez once he has seen the Eiffel Tower?" This line is most likely adapted from the First World War song "How Ya Gonna Keep 'em Down on the Farm (After They've Seen Paree?)."

This has stayed with me. It changes a person. It changes you when you are standing in front of a building once inhabited by Henry VIII and Elizabeth I. It changes you when you walk up a flight of stone stairs scalloped in the middle by a thousand years of feet walking up and down them. It changes you when you look to the ceiling of a pub, and see where Allied pilots, using either lipstick, candles or cigarette lighters, wrote their names, hometowns and squadrons before flying off to bomb Nazi Germany, many not returning. It changes you to stand beside Stonehenge and to know that humans built it thousands of years before your ancestors ever saw a white man. It changes you to see the vastness of what a city of seven million people actually looks like, at a time when your entire province didn't even have a million people in it. It changes you when, for the first real time, you experience the panoply of cultures, voices, foods, languages, sounds, smells and tastes of the larger world. I knew that I would be coming home a different man.

I was told early on by others who had travelled to Europe that, before I left, I should sew a small Canadian flag patch on everything – my backpack, my coat, my luggage, etc. When I asked why, I was simply told, "Trust me." So I did. I even went so far as to write to Hockey Canada to request a patch to sew on to my clothing. Hockey Canada, in an amazing show of generosity, actually gave me a full Team Canada hockey jersey and T-shirt, which I still have in my collection.

Growing up in Canada as an Indigenous person in the 1980s and '90s, I had not experienced any extreme Canadian patriotism. In the days before social media and the internet, with its oversaturation of American machismo, it seemed that there wasn't a need to express a sense of Canadian pride or patriotism. Also, as a descendant of those who fell under the yoke of colonial oppression, having pride in being Canadian was not a high priority. But there wasn't the proliferation of flag-waving and going out of one's way to show that you were Canadian when I was younger. Perhaps this was just my

The author as a student at the University of Cambridge, UK, July 2000. The hockey jersey was given to him by Hockey Canada for his trip.
Author's photo.

view from my somewhat sheltered and cloistered childhood spent within one city, where even a trip to Saskatoon only happened three or four times in my life.

Upon landing in the UK, however, it did not take long to discover that distinguishing myself from Americans was a very prudent thing to do. I quickly found that when it was assumed that I was American, I was met with a rather cold and disdainful air, which quickly vanished when it was learned that I was from Canada. I never paid full price for a cab fare, nor a meal in a restaurant, and had complete strangers offer to show me the sights and wonders of the British Isles. When I asked him about it, a cab driver said, in a beautifully wonderful, Michael Caine–like Cockney accent,

"Canadians, you're part of the family, now, aren't you? You're family, not like that lot. They come over here, banging around and telling everybody how bloody wonderful they are, no respect. The only thing we like about them is their money." Thinking back to the wonderful American friends I had met while living there, and to the amazing American benefactors who had taken a chance on me and made it possible for me to even be there, I felt sorry that this reputation hung over their heads. They bore no resemblance to this stereotype, and they were forced to endure it. I had Americans approach me in the street, begging me to sell them one of the Canadian flag patches on my backpack, just so they would be treated differently.

Now, this is not to say that this stereotype was completely without merit. I witnessed it first-hand many times over there. One night in particular stands out in my memory. I was sitting in a pub in Cambridge. It was a packed little pub, mostly with noisy American college students.

The students were putting coin after coin into the juke-box, playing the song "American Pie" over and over and over again, all the while drunkenly screaming the lyrics at the top of their lungs, much to the annoyance of those of us who were not American. They must have played the song five or six times.

Finally, I was able to make my way to the jukebox, and I scanned the selections. Amazingly, I saw it: "If I had $1000000" by the Barenaked Ladies. That song, in a juke-box, in a tiny hole-in-the-wall pub in England. The odds were unbelievable.

I plugged a pound coin in the jukebox and selected it. As the song began to play, I started to sing along, "If I had a million dollars…"

All of a sudden, a French-Canadian accent boomed out in response, "If I had a million dollars…" A big, tall man stood up and walked over to the jukebox.

We sang the whole song together, including the spoken interludes about Dijon ketchup.

I shook the hand of my unknown duet partner and went back to the bar. I never learned his name. I'd love to share that story with the Barenaked Ladies one day.

In retrospect, I now feel somewhat hypocritical. I was a staunch Indigenous warrior fighting colonization, who planned to stage a major protest against colonization, yet I was using that very colonial history to my advantage. It was a summer of contradictions for me, though, in so many ways.

As a light-skinned man who had to fight to be recognized in my own home territory as Indigenous, for the first time I had people coming up to me, touching my face and touching my hair, asking to have their photograph taken with a real "Red Indian." I was asked how I was getting used to running water and sleeping in a building as opposed to an igloo or a tipi, not in a racist or mean-spirited way, but because they actually and honestly believed that we as Indigenous people still lived as we had pre-contact. In as much as North American history classes were at that time still providing antiquated information about the "discoverers" of the Americas, in England there was an equally inadequate knowledge of history. This kept me on task with the mission

I had hoped to accomplish while I was there. I was going to "discover" and "claim" this land to protest what we had been taught for centuries.

Prior to leaving for England, I had connected with as many media people as I could, in order to ensure that there would be substantial news coverage. I had lined up most of the London correspondents of the Canadian news outlets, and had done a fair bit of radio and newspaper interviews before leaving and while in England (including an on-air interview with a Calgary radio station during the Calgary Stampede, with a seven hour time difference).

I had chosen the clothing I was going to wear very carefully. I wore a fringed buckskin jacket, beautifully beaded with the delicate flowers and curls that epitomize Métis beadwork. In my hand, I held a single antler from a whitetail deer, wrapped in the fur from the face of a coyote. These antlers were often used by *oskâpêwisak*, the traditional helper of Elders at ceremony, to haul the glowing red-hot rocks from the sacred fire to the sweat lodge. In my slicked back, braided hair I wore an eagle feather, gifted to me on the sacred slopes of Bear Butte in South Dakota, where I had the honour of praying prior to my journey. I looked every bit the stylized "Hollywood Indian," and this was deliberate, as this was the image that the world still had of us as Indigenous people of North America, that all "Indians" dressed in the manner of the Plains peoples, all feathers and buckskin in their movies and television shows.

Underneath the jacket, however, I wore a T-shirt, and upon that T-shirt was another image of an Indigenous man.

He was sitting, facing the same direction as the warrior on the flag. His messy hair was unkempt and chopped off at the shoulder. Wrapped around him was a tattered woollen blanket of both stripes and blocks of colour. A tobacco pipe was held in his dark-skinned left hand, and the weight of the world was shown upon his thin, wrinkled face. His right hand appeared to be resting on what looked to be a nine-pound cannon round, with a chain running from the nose of the round, out of frame, presumably to the shackle on his ankle.

The man in the photo was known in Nêhiyawak as Mistahimaskwa, or Big Bear. He was a well-known Nehiyaw Chief who resisted the signing of Treaty Six in 1876. Chief Big Bear was a figure in the 1885 North-West Rebellion, where he was arrested for treason for the role some of his warriors played in what was known as the Frog Lake Massacre, where nine white settlers were killed by warriors lead by another Chief, Wandering Spirit. While Big Bear was found to have not played a part in the massacre, nonetheless he was found guilty of treason and spent two years of a three-year sentence in Stony Mountain Penitentiary in Manitoba, and then died in poor health shortly after.

I chose to wear a shirt with Big Bear because I wanted to bring this wise man's resilience and memory with me as I took a major risk, not knowing if I too would be arrested as he was, and charged with treason, or at least trespassing. If I was to be detained at Her Majesty's pleasure in a London jail, then I wanted to make sure I had an ancestor on my side.

In the days leading up to the demonstration, I had

touched base with my media contacts and finalized the last few details. I was to join the throngs of people in front of the gates of Buckingham Palace, in full view of not only the media, but also the thousands of cameras held by thousands of tourists. I was nervous, but excited.

July 25, 2000, was a nice day in Cambridge. I was preparing to board a train to London on the morning of the twenty-seventh to stage the protest.

While I was in England, I had met a wonderful woman, and we had gotten very close very quickly. I sat in the Common Room of the dormitory building where we were staying, and I was working up the courage to ask her to come with me to London.

Suddenly, the screens of the BBC flashed a special report. That afternoon, a Concorde jet, with 109 people aboard, crashed after takeoff in Paris, killing everyone on board as well as four more people on the ground.

The room went silent, with only slight gasps, or the utterance of an occasional "oh my God."

I was shocked by the loss, when I suddenly came to my senses, and a foreboding feeling came over me.

I rushed out of the room and dashed to the bank of public telephones in the foyer. I pulled out the list of media numbers from my pocket and dialed the first one.

"Hey, it's John McDonald. Listen, are we still good for Thursday?"

A pause, then, "Listen, I don't think we're going to be able to make it. With the crash, all of our resources are going to be tied up for a while. I'm sorry."

It was the same story with every contact person. There would be no media coverage on the ground. In the grand scheme of things, a news story about one guy being a shit disturber a long way from home paled in comparison to the tragic loss of so many lives in such a fiery way.

That night, the wonderful woman I had met wrapped her arms around my shoulder. "So, what are you going to do?" she asked.

I looked up at the flag, where it hung on the wall of my room. "I said I was going to do it," I said, "and I'm going to do it."

At 11:30 a.m. British Summer Time (5:30 a.m. back home), I walked from my lodgings, down Sidgwick Avenue and into the park behind Queens' College. I had decided not to go to London, where, without the legitimacy of the media being present, my actions would have been lost among the masses and nothing achieved. I had decided to stay in Cambridge for this. I chose creating a moderate stir in one of the beating hearts of history.

There were many stares as I walked down the sidewalk, the flag fluttering behind me from a long piece of wooden dowelling I had absconded with from one of the local laboratories. I thought of all the people who had given me so much and taken such a huge risk on sending me here. I thought of my grandfathers, the biological one I had never met and the step-grandfather I knew and loved all my life. They had both walked upon English soil during the Second World War, both Indigenous men a long way from home for the first time. I remembered my step-grandfather telling me of

The author preparing to "claim" England, standing before the former gates of Newnham College, University of Cambridge, UK, July 27, 2000.
Author's photo.

the time when his unit stood in formation upon Blackfriars Bridge in London, when King George VI inspected them. I remembered what he said he could see and hear from where he stood.

As I crossed the street and into the crowded grassy park on that summer's afternoon, I felt the eyes of those lazily reading books and eating their lunches gazing at me. A small crowd began to gather around the small core group of classmates and new friends I had invited and cajoled into witnessing the event.

I began to sing a ceremonial song, with no drum or rattle. I sang it softly and nervously at first, but slowly grew louder.

I had my eyes shut as I sang, sure that when I opened them, there would be nobody there.

I finished my song, opened my eyes and saw that a few more curious people had joined the group.

I cleared my throat, and began to speak.

"My friends, I have travelled many thousands of kilometres and have landed upon these shores, where I was met by its ancestral inhabitants.

"I look around, and I see a people with their own civilization, their own language, their own communities, their own buildings and religion and way of life.

"In the time-honoured tradition of Christopher Columbus, John Cabot, Jacques Cartier, Hernán Cortés and so many others who came to our homeland, I say that none of this existed before my arrival, and that everything I see here now, I am the first 'civilized' person to see, and thus I have discovered it, and in the name of the Creator, and for all of the inhabitants of Turtle Island, the Americas and the Caribbean, I hereby claim this land for us.

"Remember this, my friends: You cannot 'discover' something when someone is already there. You did not 'discover' us – we were not lost. You did not 'conquer' us – we are not conquered. Hoka hey."

I planted the flag into the ground and bowed my head.

I wish that I could say that, like in the movies, there was silence, then one person clapping, then two, then, as the momentum builds, the applause became deafening. However, it wasn't like that. There was, as I love to say, a smattering of tepid applause, and then the crowd dispersed. There were no questions asked, no one shook my hand in congratulations. It was over.

I was lucky that one of the people I had invited to witness the event had offered to take photos of me with my disposable camera, so that there was, indeed, proof that it had happened. I thanked them, took my camera back and walked back to my room.

A few days after I returned to Canada, I met with a reporter from my local newspaper, who wanted to do a story about "the Flag Thing," as he put it. I agreed, and the story was printed the next day.

However, the story was also picked up by the Canadian Press wire service, where it quickly made the rounds of many Canadian newspapers. While it wasn't necessarily front-page news for many of these papers, it began to build a life of its own, reaching the American wire service and, since it was 2000, the early internet news websites. Suddenly, the story of the "Cree Indian" who "discovered" England for the First Peoples of the Americas went relatively global, though often it was printed in the "In Other News" section towards the back of the paper. One newspaper went so far as to refer to it, tongue-in-cheek, as "The Empire Strikes Back."

The biggest impact for me personally, however, was felt in the grassroots Indigenous communities, both on-reserve and in urban settings. I was instantly recognized and lauded as the guy who "did the Flag Thing" by people on the street. When I would go into Indigenous communities and into schools, I was always introduced as "the guy who went over to England and claimed it for *us*." There would be hugs and expressions of gratitude for an act that, in spite of a lack of media coverage when it happened, has lived on through being passed from person to person via oral storytelling. I have been fortunate to have shared this story hundreds of times to thousands of people on stages across Canada, the United States and even Australia – where I was presented with an Australian flag signed by the then Governor-General of Australia. For twenty years, the tale has continued, and a month doesn't go by when someone doesn't bring it up. It is still being shared by both Indigenous and non-Indigenous people.

For nearly half of the twenty years since the event, the flag sat folded in the bottom of an old steamer trunk I inherited from my grandfather, under piles of photo albums and other ephemera. The jacket I had worn was donated to the local historical museum, and the deer antler was gifted away long ago. The Big Bear T-shirt also is gone, fallen apart and tattered after years of use.

When I turned thirty, I had a major health scare that suddenly delivered many rude awakenings, one of which was the fact that a time will come when I will not be around to share the story of the flag and the events of that summer. I wanted to ensure that others would be able to see it and hear the tale long after I was gone.

Around the tenth anniversary of the event, I entrusted the flag to the care of the Canadian Museum of History.

The year 2020 marked the twentieth anniversary of the "discovery" and "claiming" of England. I had hoped that, perhaps, I might be able to return to that grassy park along the banks of the River Cam and recreate the event, and perhaps travel to Ottawa to see my old friend once again. Sadly, as the major news story that was the Concorde crash had diverted attention away from the event the first time, the COVID-19 pandemic repeated this a second time. One day, when the world has settled into some sort of new normalcy that will allow travel once again, we will gather again, and those truths uttered that day will ring out again: You cannot "discover" something when someone is already there. You did not "discover" us – we were not lost. You did not "conquer" us – we are not conquered.

The Verdict

When I heard the verdict, I was standing in sight of the spot where Leo LaChance was murdered in Prince Albert, Saskatchewan, by a white supremacist in January 1991.

I walked the few hundred steps to the bronze memorial statue that stands near the site. I trembled in the frozen air, staring into those cold bronze eyes. I had no tobacco to put down, but I stood, and I wept.

As I stood there alone that night, in the shadow of a courthouse ironically, perhaps poetically, erected over the site of Leo LaChance's murder, I knew I had to say something.

It is the role of an *otâcimow*, a storyteller, to share the stories. It is also the role of a *nôtinikêwiyiniw*, a warrior, to defend the helpless and those who cannot defend themselves. These are the roles I must fulfill, because they were entrusted to me, but they are not why I wrote this. I wrote this as a human being, grieving the senseless and brutal murder of a young man, a boy who now lies beneath the snow and earth in the graveyard of Red Pheasant Reserve, a young man who can no longer speak for himself, but who has a nation of grieving, angry voices speaking for him.

This trial should have been Saskatchewan's Nuremberg – Saskatchewan's chance to mete out justice for crimes against humanity, to serve notice that racism, xenophobia and right-wing conservative hatred should not and will not have a place in our society. Instead, this has become Saskatchewan's Rodney King – where even overwhelming evidence was no match for the fact that when a person of colour is attacked by someone with privilege, be it the colour of their skin or the badge on their chest, the chances of justice for that person are almost non-existent.

My people have lived within a one-hundred-kilometre radius of the city of Prince Albert for at least thirteen thousand years. Thirteen millennia. This land is part of my DNA, this land has always been here. Yet I found myself living in fear of being murdered...in Canada...in 2018. When Colten Boushie was murdered, the saddest question I heard came from an Indigenous elementary school student, who asked, "Is there anywhere in Canada where people don't hate us?" It broke my heart, because I could not give this child an answer. I'm now asking the same question myself, and, to be honest, I do not think such a place exists. For nearly twenty years, I have lived in a small rural community, serving that community as a firefighter and first responder. I have saved the lives and property of many of those people near me, putting my life on the line and suffering the effects of PTSD in the process. After the verdict, some of those same people openly joked about me now having to "be careful" if my car ever broke down near their place.

Now what is justice? What do you deem just? Is it an eye for an eye? What justice can be made from this? Justice has not been served in this case, nor the murder of Leo LaChance, nor the murder of Pamela George, nor the rape of a twelve-year-old Indigenous girl in Tisdale, Saskatchewan, nor the murder of Tina Fontaine, nor the murders and disappearances of thousands of Indigenous women and men, and I could go on.

I asked myself, "What justice would serve the killer Gerald Stanley?" It started with that – referring to him as "the Killer." Fred Goldman, the father of Ron Goldman, the young man murdered alongside Nicole Brown Simpson, will rarely, if ever, be heard referring to O.J. Simpson as anything but "the killer" or "the murderer." I took my first lesson from him.

Justice for the Killer had already begun. He has been painted with the brush of notoriety. He will always be known as "the killer of Colten Boushie." Wherever he goes, his name is cursed by his actions. He will carry it for the rest of his days. His family will carry it, his son will carry it and his grandchildren will carry it. His family will forever be marked in Saskatchewan as "the family of the killer."

What justice did I want meted out?

I thought long and carefully before I put pen to paper. I weighed each word carefully, for I knew that I would have to take responsibility for every single word I said. I smudged, I wept and I wrote.

I wanted the Killer to have every waking moment of his life scarred by what he did. I wanted the memories of that day to always be on his mind. I wanted him to not have a minute's peace, as he replayed that day over and over again. I wanted the Killer to never have a moment's rest. I wanted him tossing and turning in his bed, unable to sleep, his nightmares vivid and visceral, terrifying and real. I wanted him to forever look at that spot in his driveway and be reminded of it, over and over and over again.

I wanted the Killer to be ostracized by society. I wanted people to be made uncomfortable in his presence. When he walked into a business, I wanted people to get up and leave. I wanted people to cross the street and walk on the other side of the street as he approached. I wanted him followed around by store security in every establishment he entered. I wanted him to be asked to leave restaurants and stores because his very presence in the business was unsettling for the other customers. I wanted mothers shielding their children from him.

I wanted the Killer's property to become a tourist location. I wanted carloads of gawkers and rubberneckers stopping at his property, gaggles of them, at all hours. I wanted marches and ceremonies to be held in the road allowances. I wanted his neighbours to be inconvenienced by all of this. I wanted his neighbours to become angry at him for bringing all of this to their quiet rural life. I wanted the property he felt so desperate to defend to become such an uncomfortable place to be that he should have no peace there. I wanted the Killer's property to no longer be a refuge for him.

I wanted the Killer to have his crime brought up at every moment he tried to interact with anyone. I wanted his entire life defined by the fact that he killed someone. I wanted people to say, "Aren't you the guy who murdered that guy?" I wanted the topic of murder brought up every time the Killer is in conversation. I wanted the Killer to have it constantly thrown in his face that he killed someone.

I wanted the Killer to find it hard to make a living. I wanted his ability to put food on his table compromised. I wanted the Killer to be refused work, to be denied income. I wanted the Killer to be forced into such destitution that all the crowdsourcing pages set up by equally xenophobic individuals combined wouldn't be able to save him, and he would be forced to lose every precious object he possessed.

What I did not want, however, was for the Killer to be physically harmed or killed, and if you have carefully read what I have written here, not once do I call for any violent repercussions.

There is no need for violence towards the Killer, his family or his supporters. Not only is it wrong, but violence and hatred are the reason why Colten Boushie lies in his grave. I have spent the many months following the verdict meditating on the works of Cesar Chavez and Dr. Martin Luther King Jr., and I adhere to their doctrines of non-violence. You see, my justice would have been cold, long-term and, for the Killer, 100 percent self-inflicted.

Alas, Saskatchewan being as it is, often referred to online as the "Mississippi or Alabama of the North," none of this came to pass. It appears as if the Killer has fled the place over which he felt the need to kill. He is now somewhere in obscurity with funds gathered through his supporters. Every time it is mentioned in the news, the online comments are filled with those of privilege asking, "It's over and done with. Quit bringing it up all the time. Why can't you just leave it alone?"

Why? Because Colten Boushie lies beneath the soil of Red Pheasant, way before his time.

Two Roads

I am Nêhiyawak-Métis. I come from a point of privilege that my grandparents are well-known historical figures in Métis history. I recognize that. I've been deeply fortunate to have learned so much over the past few years, with many lessons and many teachings gifted in many different ways by many different teachers.

The most important of these lessons, however, if I can be truly honest, have been the lessons that I learned regarding the two worlds in which I walk – the First Nations world and the Métis world – and the delicate balance therein.

I come from a lineage thousands of years old, filled with resilient women and men who, in some of the harshest environments and situations on earth, not merely survived, but thrived. The Irish and Scottish blood I carry felt the yoke of British colonialist oppression far longer than my Indigenous blood. I cannot pick and choose which ancestors to honour. I honour them all.

The past few years have seen me reconnecting and more deeply exploring my Métis heritage, once again delving into the legends of my family: The great-great-grandfather who fought alongside Riel during the Red River Uprising, fled west and made his home on the land now known as Edmonton. The great-great-grandmother who, in a moment of genius and quick thinking, saved my great-great-grandfather from being convicted and hung as a Métis spy. The great-grandfather who came to Canada from the Irish upper class, but walked away from the money for the love of a Métis woman, who in time, became the first Métis registered nurse in Alberta. Of course, there is my own grandfather, one of the greatest leaders in Métis history.

As proud as I am of my Nêhiyawak heritage, I am equally as proud of my Métis blood. I am truly blessed to come from both. These are not merely interchangeable hats that I put on depending where I am to suit the situation. This is who I am every day – with one foot on the Red Road and the other in the tracks of the Red River cart. But the fact that I am both was a major lesson I had to learn.

Now, at this point, I would be remiss if I did not address difficult truths about the historical relationship between Indigenous and Métis people. In 1976, a book was written entitled *Kātāayuk: Saskatchewan Indian Elders*, which was a collection of stories and teachings from Elders in Treaty Six Territory gathered during the hundredth anniversary year of the signing of Treaty Six.

My grandmother had a copy of this book, and it was a book I spent much time as a kid poring over, staring at the black-and-white photographs, and trying to decipher the burgundy-coloured Cree syllabics written underneath the testimonies of these Elders. It was one of my first inroads into the oral storytelling traditions of my people, and many of the Elders interviewed are relations of mine.

One of the Elders who spoke was Solomon Johnstone, from the Mistawasis Reserve, which is my mother's home community. It is in his telling of the 1885 Resistance where the mythology of Louis Riel first came into question for me and his words caused a great deal of contemplation on my part over the years.

In his story, he talks about how word of the Battle of Duck Lake first reached the Mistawasis band, and how messengers were sent to the nearby reserves to pass on the information. There was discussion of joining the resistance, as other bands had. Poundmaker himself was a nephew of Chief Mistawasis.

As it had been less than ten years since Chief Mistawasis and his cousin Ahtahkakoop had first signed Treaty Six, they chose not to join the fight on either side, and instead chose to honour their treaty with the queen. They left their reserves and lead the people to the east, where they set up camp with two other bands to wait out the summer.

At some point, Riel sent two messengers to this new camp to try and enlist the warriors to join the fight. The leaders informed the Métis messengers that their warriors would not fight against the queen, nor would they fight for her. They wanted to stay out of the fight for the sake of the old people. They were assured by the Métis messengers that they would be left alone.

When the Mistawasis and Ahtahkakoop bands returned to their reserves that summer, after the fighting was over, they discovered that their houses had been destroyed in retaliation for not joining the fight.

I was very young when I first read this passage, and I didn't really possess the ability then to process it. At some point in my youth, I attached the idea that the houses were burned to the story, though I have no basis in fact that the homes were destroyed by fire. For all I know, they were pulled down. But with the few fires that had been set by Métis "envoys" during the so-called Siege of Battleford, where the white population of the area huddled inside the walls of the fort at Battleford, waiting for an "Indian uprising" that never occurred, I probably jumped to the conclusion that the homes on the Mistawasis and Atahkakoop reserves were set to the torch.

As time went on, however, my reading and research allowed me to put it all into a better context, and, knowing the value of oral storytelling from the perspective of an Elder, the odds of it being a made-up tale are slim. Confirmation of the story later came as I read Blair Stonechild and Bill Waiser's 1997 book, *Loyal till Death: Indians and the North-West Rebellion*, and learned for the first time of the tactics employed by some of the Métis in order to get Indigenous warriors to join the fight on the side of the Métis, including, ironically, utilizing starvation in order to coerce the warriors to fight, which was a strategy Ottawa had used time and again in an attempt to gain complete control over the Indigenous people.

With the structure of Métis leadership during the time of the 1885 Resistance, it seems likely to me that the order to destroy the houses would have come from only two people – Gabriel Dumont or Louis Riel. It is entirely possible that the destruction of the houses was done solely upon impulse of the Métis emissaries.

I also learned that Riel held less than sympathetic views towards the First Nations people. As Stonechild and Waiser state in their book, "Riel regarded the Indians as a simple, primitive people, who should be made to

Louis Riel.
Library and Archives Canada, C-018082 / Bibliothèque et Archives Canada, C-018082.

work 'as Pharaoh had made the Jews work.' He also assumed that the Métis, because of their mixed-blood parentage, could help solve the so-called Indian problem – in his words, 'show them how to earn their living' – by exercising a positive and uplifting influence upon them."

This information shattered the almost religious mythology of Riel for me, and brought him back down to human level, with human attributes – vindictive, sanctimonious and deceitful. However, it is often said that the first casualty of war is the truth, so perhaps it is to be taken with a grain of salt.

During a recent conversation with a colleague, I gave a somewhat oversimplified summation of this particular aspect of my collective past. I referred to the history of this particular relationship as "a chronicle of some of the horrible things some of my Métis relations did to my Nêhiyawak relations while combating the assholes sent from Ottawa by that King of the Assholes who had the same name as me" (referring to that "other" John A). As I have always said, history is ugly. If history is pretty, then a whole bunch of the story is being left out. When it comes to Louis Riel himself, he is still, by virtue of time and precedence, a folk hero, and is becoming more and more like Robin Hood as the decades pass. The man vanishes but the myth remains.

I am quickly approaching that stage of life known as middle-aged. I spent the first half of my life fighting to be accepted, recognized and welcomed as a First Nations man. From residential school to my role as a Knowledge Carrier, it has not been easy, and, being light-skinned, that fight has always been uphill.

As I move towards the "second half," as it were, the path towards reconnecting with my Métis heritage seems to be filled with less resistance, if not much easier, if that makes sense. I am not saying that I am walking away from my Nêhiyawak heritage or responsibilities, but I do feel that a greater amount of my personal time will be spent building those bridges once again with my Bois-Brûlé bloodline, lending my voice to the Infinity flag and continuing the legacy and the fight of my grandparents.

Why continue the fight?

I have stood on the steps of the church at Batoche and looked south towards the battlefield many times, as I'm sure

Louis Riel had done many times. I have closed my eyes and tried to put myself in that man's shoes, hearing the sharp cracks of musket fire from the pits and the returning thunder of artillery, knowing that the ammunition will soon be gone and that those men with whom he had prayed and broken bread a few days earlier would soon be loading their guns with stones and nails to fight back against cannon and Gatling gun.

I wonder at what point he saw the tide turn and knew that the ground war was lost. I think he knew at that point, however, that the fight had only just begun.

In the unique position I hold, the descendant of ancestors who played such pivotal roles during the chaotic and emotionally charged history of this province, it would be remiss of me to stand to the side and say nothing about the current state of affairs concerning the issues facing both Indigenous and Métis peoples. Indeed, many of the issues faced in those cold days of 1885 have never been resolved, and the legacy of mistrust, of isolationism, of "us against them, and them also," is one which has weighed heavily upon my mind for a long time, compounding the internal struggle I have often faced regarding my advocacy and how to use it.

As is, sadly, often the case when it comes to the charged relationship between First Nations and Métis peoples, painful, hateful and disgusting comments are often posted online going back and forth between the two groups. Many times, the conversation turns to the age-old pissing contest of how much of something you are; how much of your ancestry is Métis, how much of you is First Nations, how dark is your skin, how blond is your hair, how blue are your eyes and on and on. The tit-for-tat often turns ugly, violent, threatening and, ultimately, racist. The funny thing is, both sides claim to be trying to work for the same thing: ensuring the strength and integrity of their respective nations.

It is terrifyingly similar to the arguments often made by white supremacists, fighting to keep this ridiculous concept of bloodlines "pure." Too many times, I shake my head in absolute disgust at some of the conversations, and I shake it even harder when these conversations are being held by individuals in positions of authority, elected or otherwise, or by individuals in positions of respect and honour. Long ago, I made a decision to remove the words *they should know better* from my vocabulary, because I do not know where people are coming from in terms of upbringing and education. However, there have been too many times over the past few years where I have wanted to say this.

While it is one thing to speak out against cultural appropriation, and to be an advocate for the protection of the rights and culture of an Indigenous people, to spew such hate and anger is beyond reprehensible.

Hatred and condemnation for individuals of mixed ancestry, along with the calling for "pure blood," is literally straight out of Hitler's playbook. They are the tenets of the Nuremberg Laws of 1935. These beliefs led to the creation of concentration and extermination camps, as well as the death of millions of innocent people.

Indigenous people of mixed ancestry, along with members of the Métis Nation, have faced hatred, ostracism, violence and even threats of extermination, and continue to do so today. As a light-skinned Indigenous person, I have been ridiculed, ostracized and labelled as somehow "less than" within the Indigenous community because of the lightness of my skin.

This needs to stop.

This being said, I must speak to a current issue in Eastern Canada and the Maritimes, where groups of individuals who have some Indigenous ancestry are gathering together to refer to themselves as "Eastern Métis" or "Acadian Métis." This is a phenomenon that seems to have begun due to the recent Supreme Court cases that have opened up new avenues for funding and hunting and fishing rights for Métis people.

In the United States, there is something I call the "Cherokee princess" effect. To make themselves more palatable or exotic to others, some Americans will claim to have a "Cherokee princess" in their family tree. It has become a trope and, to the detriment of the actual Cherokee people, when someone claims Cherokee ancestry, eyes in the Indigenous community roll derisively.

Some non-Indigenous people think that because they have Indigenous ancestry, they can claim to be Métis. Some Indigenous people think that because they have European ancestry, they can claim to be Métis. For many Métis, including myself, this alone does not make you Métis. Being Métis isn't about having an Indigenous or European ancestor in your family tree. The word *Métis* is not a catch-all for individuals who have mixed-Indigenous heritage.

The definition of *Métis* is, and has been for most of the past two hundred years, that you have strong familial connections to either the original nineteenth-century Plains buffalo hunting societies and communities, or to the northern fur trapping communities of Manitoba, Saskatchewan and Alberta. It is about having strong and deep connections to the culture, language and history of the Métis, as well as being recognized and accepted as a member of long-established Métis communities.

I recognize that there are people out there desperately searching for a cultural identity, who feel that because of some familial connection, they can claim to be Métis. My heart aches for their personal cultural loss, but this alone does not make one Métis.

When non-Métis individuals begin to claim Métis heritage without a connection to the Métis Nation, be it for access to financial gain, access to Métis rights and opportunities, or simply because it's trendy, it erodes the nearly two centuries of determination, resistance, military combat and indescribable hard work that our ancestors put in to have us recognized as a distinct Indigenous people in this land.

This is also a tremendous slap in the face to the thousands of survivors of the Sixties Scoop, who were stolen as children and infants from their homes and had that familial connection forcibly broken by being adopted into white families. When these people have had to fight through years of colonialist trauma and abuse to reconnect with a heritage ripped from their arms, to have someone cavalierly come along and say, "Oh, by the way, I should be part of this because of some distant ancestor," is cruel, and is perpetuating the colonization of those individuals.

Over the past few years, the number of individuals who have sought to gain grant funding, employment and media attention by claiming Indigenous ancestry has grown, as have community leaders speaking up to ensure that these are honest claims, calling out those who are engaging in dishonesty.

In Indigenous culture, we seek out kinship and connectivity. When someone says that they have a connection to a certain community, it is our nature to enquire as to that connection: "Who's your mom? Who was your grandmother? What's the family name?" This serves a dual role in providing context and connectivity – where does this person fit into the community story – as well as a form of, to borrow a phrase from one of my aunties, "finding out if they're full of shit." A majority of the time, people are accepted into the fold, even if the familial connection is somewhat tenuous. It is a matter of trust and seeking kinship connections to ensure that those who belong in the circle are accepted and recognized.

Too often, we as Indigenous people have been duped. Too often, our trust and support has been violated in order to further someone's agenda and make a name or money off our backs. Again and again, major successes have been stolen by someone pretending to be something that they are not, someone who can tell, as George Carlin said, "a good bullshit story."

When this happens, it is impossible for us as Indigenous communities to not tighten our circle and eye with suspicion those trying their best to break into our sacredness.

We are hurt. We are wounded. It hurts to be conned by someone we brought in.

I have always believed that one should allow oneself to feel this pain. We should honour it for the lessons and teachings it brings. Do not deny the pain. Acknowledge this pain and add it to the resilience upon which our people have thrived for thousands of years.

We overcame it when a particular award-winning author who shall remain nameless claimed Indigenous heritage and began to take up a space that should have rightly been filled by someone with closer ties to tell the stories, just as we did with Grey Owl before him.

We have overcome every person who has claimed a Cherokee princess as an ancestor. We will overcome the "Eastern Métis" and those who hope to bulldoze their way into the legacy fought for and died for at Batoche.

As I write this, another well-known individual in the media who has garnered great success by telling Indigenous stories without really having an honest connection to an Indigenous community has come to light. They are being called out for filling a space that should have been filled with someone more entitled to tell those stories, and the Indigenous community, once again, is leading that call. I suspect that we will continue to do so for a very long time. I imagine that the number of "pretendians," as they are becoming known, will continue to rise.

As I have done always, I fully acknowledge the privilege I have in terms of knowing my lineage and coming from the family that I do. Through my mother, I can draw a straight and direct line of lineage to Chief Mistawasis, my three times great-grandfather (my great-grandfather's grandfather). My mother's home community is the Mistawasis Nêhiyawak.

Through my paternal grandmother, I am descended from Chief Petequakey, and I am a recognized and accepted member of the Muskeg Lake Cree Nation, as was my late father, and as are my children.

My mother and my late father, along with myself, and my sisters, are residential school survivors.

Through my own grandfather, I can draw a direct line to both the Métis settlement of St.-Paul-des-Métis and the original Red River Settlement. My great-great-grandfather fought alongside Riel in the first uprising

Also through my grandfather, I can draw a line of lineage to County Cavan, Ireland, where his own father was born, and through my Dreaver line, I can draw a line to Papa Westray, Orkney, Scotland, to a Viking-Scottish bloodline that goes back to paleolithic times.

I was born in, and as a young boy I grew up surrounded by, the strong urban Indigenous community of P.A., and I was mentored and brought into

The author's great-great-great-grandfather Chief Mistawasis is seated on the right side of the image.

"Peter Hourie and Indian Chiefs." Saskatchewan Archives Board R-B2837.

our cultural teachings and way of life by the late Elders Vicki Wilson, Rita Parenteau, Laura Merasty, John James Daniels (Ironswing) and William Turner. They helped me revive the way of life that five years of living in a residential school tried to destroy.

Each morning, I remember this heritage, and I think about these ancestors whose gift of life brought me here. I thank them each morning in quiet reflection, and I acknowledge how lucky I am to have had the ability to do so.

I also have to acknowledge that one of the reasons why I know my lineage so well, and reference it as often as I do, is because I am often required to prove my Indigenous ancestry against accusations of not being "Indigenous enough." Too often, I have to recite my family tree to those who question me because of my light skin, lest I be labelled a "pretendian." I am always aware that the privilege I have in knowing my heritage as well as I do comes from the fact that it is under constant scrutiny.

For those of us whose lines are etched forever in stone, we must remember those whose lines were etched in sand at the water's edge, and who had a wave come along and erase it, so that only a ghost of a depression remained.

The Métis Nation is not some trendy, New Age club to join in an attempt to make yourself seem exotic, nor is it a catch-all for everybody with mixed ancestry. The Métis Nation is a distinct people, based around a rich and colourfully nuanced history stemming from those who created beautiful lives and communities in such places as along the Red River, Batoche, Green Lake and St.-Paul-des-Métis.

Is there a way forward through all of this? Perhaps.

As this struggle continues to unfold, as with anything, those of us involved, or at least remotely interested in the subject, are ultimately called upon to take sides. It often feels like, and one could surmise that it is similar to, the envoys who went out from both sides of the resistance in 1885, assaying where loyalties laid. As it stands, there does not appear to be a simple, bipartisan approach for someone to sit on the fence or to engage in whatever euphemisms are needed to show that you are trying very hard to be diplomatic and sympathetic to both sides. The emotional involvement is deep, and there are many ways in which whatever is said either way can be misconstrued. We must all tread carefully going forward.

The Photograph

There is a black-and white photograph that has been floating around on social media for some time.

It is a photograph taken, one would assume, at some point in the 1950s or 1960s. In the foreground of the photo three nuns stand in full habits, each holding a newborn baby. Behind the nuns stand an Indigenous man and woman. They appear to be in a room within a hospital, as the door behind them has a hydraulic door closer. In the bottom right-hand corner of the photograph stands a table with a white cloth, upon which stands a white pillar candle and a thin book. One would assume that the photo was taken at the time of a baptism.

The faces of these nuns, three white women, reveal a smugness, a look of authority. The faces of the couple behind them, however, speak volumes; they are the faces of shock, of exhaustion, of doubt and of uncertainty.

I am the father of one of the rare sets of Indigenous triplets in Canada. Every time I see this photo, it guts me. I look into the faces of those parents, and I see the fears of myself and my partner. I see our shock, exhaustion, overwhelming emotions and uncertainty reflected back at me, that knowing that your world and your family has changed forever. But to watch as your newborn children are being indoctrinated into a foreign belief system must have been a nightmare. Though, if the parents themselves willingly allowed this to happen, then this photograph is even more heartbreaking as it shows the multi-generational loss of culture at the hands of colonialism, something I have experienced first-hand and have worked all my life to correct.

I would like to find out the backstory of this photo. Is this indeed a set of triplets? Were they taken from their parents? Where are they today?

When I look at this photo, I cannot help but look into myself, not only as a parent, but as someone who can quite easily project my own emotions and experiences into it. It caused me to do some deep introspective realization, moving further towards better understanding my own traumas and idiosyncrasies, learning my own triggers and dealing with them accordingly as they come up, acknowledging them in the attempt to move past them. A major trigger for me is what many people refer to as "misbehaving" children: kids running around in public spaces, screaming, causing havoc, essentially being kids. A child yelling and not listening to their parents or teachers creates a huge amount of anxiety in me. I experienced very personally the maxim of "children should be seen and not heard." I had that mentality drummed into me, programmed deeply into me, and it took quite a long time to override my knee-jerk reaction to correct or discipline a child for rowdy behaviour, or to look at it as a sign that the parents weren't "doing their job" in terms of their child's behaviour.

I've learned to control my anxiety to the point where it rarely manifests, but there was a night a few years ago when a group of children running around noisily while someone was performing onstage at an event triggered me to the point where I had to hide in a bathroom stall and control my breathing. I was going into complete "fight or flight." I wanted to run.

There are many posts online that feel that the children of today would be much better behaved if their parents "disciplined them," which basically means to beat the child into obedience. On the complete opposite end of that spectrum are parents who provide no discipline or consequences to their children whatsoever, and who are guilty of willfully ignoring their children's behaviours or actions.

My children are now, as of this writing, in their teens. They are, for the most part, respectful, mature and responsible young people, intelligent and dependable, with few of the foibles that are expected of a teenager. When I hear people compliment me on the behaviour of my children, on how respectful and pleasant they are, I feel a sense of pride in them, but also pride in myself as a parent. And I fully admit to feeling a bit of smug superiority over those parents whose children are raising hell in the stores and whose teenagers hate them, but that is simply a continuation of the cycle of that old maxim "children are to be seen and not heard," and

I acknowledge that. We all feel, as parents, that our children's behaviour is a reflection on our parenting. What's missing from this, however, is the acknowledgement that our children are individuals themselves, with their own thoughts, feelings, personalities and emotions, and that their behaviour is dictated by them based on the examples provided to them at all times and from all quarters. We as parents are not the sole models for our children's behaviour, but we are a major part of how they live their lives.

I remember early on in my career working with "at-risk" youth, I would smile whenever someone would ask me why I wanted to work with "those" kids. I knew what they meant, of course, by their condescending remark, so I would smile.

I would smile, because the smile would stop me from demanding of the person, "What do you mean by 'those' kids? What are you insinuating by referring to them as 'those' kids? Are they somehow different from other children, or are they themselves, in your eye, the 'other'? Have you marked them as 'other' based upon the standards by which you have set out? Please explain it to me!"

"These standards," I want to ask, "are they devised by those in, as the euphemism goes, 'a higher socio-economic bracket'? Are they 'those' kids because they are poor? Are they 'those' kids because they are hungry? Or is it much simpler than that?"

You do not need to read between too many lines to see that, too many times, they are deemed "those" kids simply because of the colour of their skin, the last name they have or the neighbourhood they are in.

They are seen as "those" kids because of the struggles that they have faced, struggles and pain over which they themselves have no control, and they are deemed to be "those" kids because of the way that they react to their pain and their struggles.

No, I get it, you deem them "those" kids, because you see them as "bad" kids.

You see them as "those" kids because they "don't listen." They are "always in trouble," they are "up to no good."

Yes, I see the point that you are trying to make, the insinuation that, somehow, because you yourself cannot imagine a situation where "those" kids can bring you any feeling other than the fear of what they might do, it must be true that devoting any significant amount of time trying to helping them find their way around the obstacles the world has placed in front of them is, in fact, wasted time.

Now, while I could say all this to them, I would come off as an "angry Indian" on the attack. So I choose not to because of that, and I choose not to because I know that I cannot change those minds until they themselves are willing to change. So I smile, and when they ask me why I want to work with those kids, I reply with a short and sweet little answer.

"Why? Because I was one of 'those' kids."

When I was a kid, my father took my little sister and me into a store. My father was very dark skinned, and my little sister and I are not. We were followed the whole time because the store clerk thought, "This Indian is trying to kidnap these little kids." We were, if memory serves me correctly, detained by store staff and eventually let go. I cannot even begin to imagine the emotions that my father must have felt in this situation. He could not have become angry, because, once again, the "angry and violent Indian" prejudice would have certainly gotten us taken away and him arrested. He must have been so embarrassed, so angry, that he was not recognized as the father of his own children. He would have had to keep his emotions in check, and he would have had to genuflect to these individuals, appeasing them and convincing them that he really was our father, doing nothing more than taking his own children to the store.

During my teenage years, I was always followed around in stores – I had long hair in a braid and wore a bandana – and I was kicked out of stores all the time, always told, "You're not stealing anything from here, now leave." To this day, when I walk into a store, my head is on a swivel, watching for staff watching me, hypervigilant from years of experience.

This is one of the realities of being Indigenous in Saskatchewan – in the eyes of retail workers, we are all thieves because of our race, and we are to be watched like hawks because we can't be trusted.

Does theft happen? Absolutely. Is some of that theft perpetrated by Indigenous individuals? Yes, sadly. As an Indigenous man, it is a painful experience watching another Indigenous man being searched by store security. It's even more painful to watch as store security pull stolen merchandise out of his coat and backpack.

While my children are light-skinned, and have the privilege of "white-passing," we've still had to have the same talk with them that every Black and Indigenous parent has had to have with their children at some point – the conversation and the lessons needed to avoid being singled out in a store and assumed to be a shoplifter. "Keep your hands out of your pockets, don't touch items on the shelves, don't go into a store unless you've got money to pay for stuff, look around but don't 'look around,'" and so on.

Yes, when in stores with my children, I am followed to this day. My children have seen it, and I have experienced what my father felt so long ago.

I remember one weekend, my teenage daughter and I witnessed the open and everyday blatant racism of the city near where we live, this time in a walk-in medical location, where an Indigenous man, bleeding from what appeared to be recent dental surgery, politely asked if he could use the washroom to simply rinse the blood from his mouth and change the dressing. The receptionist coldly told him, "No, I'm not cleaning that up. Try the gas station across the street." The man was not rude, nor was he belligerent. He was in distress, and was looking for a bit of compassion, a bit of humanity, perhaps a bit of privacy. Instead, as a man in need of some minor medical assistance, he was essentially told to leave a Walk-in Minor Emergency Medical Clinic and to change surgical dressings in a gas station bathroom.

I stood to say something, but another patient, a younger white woman in the waiting room, beat me to it. "You didn't need to be such a bitch! He was looking for help! You should've just let him use the washroom!" The receptionist replied, "Well, they always come in and make a mess of the

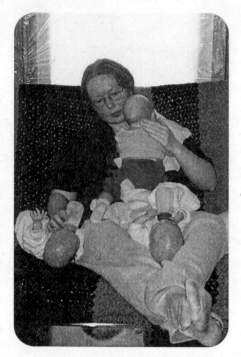

Sarah McDonald feeding triplets, 2008.
Author's photo.

washroom, these people." I wanted to jump in, but, like my father before me, the threat of the "angry Indian" stereotype and having the cops called and my daughter taken away was strong. Before I had a chance to think of what to do, we were called into the doctor's office. By the time we got out, both the receptionist and the woman in the waiting room were gone. I wish I could have thanked that woman in the waiting room. She stepped up as an ally, speaking up for this young man. She didn't have to, but I am so glad that she did.

That afternoon, I phoned the administration of that location to address what happened, and, though I was initially gaslit, I got what amounted to a "we'll look into it."

That night, I checked in with my daughter. I wanted to debrief with her, to check in with her emotions about this and to explain the dismissive reply I received from the place. I asked my daughter how she felt about this, that essentially nothing will really be done, and that this happens every day, everywhere, to Indigenous people.

"Disappointed," she said.

"Me, too," I replied. This is one of the many realities of being an Indigenous person in Canada.

I also have a photograph. It was taken when our triplets were less than a year old, still babies, eating breast milk from bottles. Remember, there were three babies and, the last time I checked, my wife has only two nipples. We had an eighteen-month-old daughter at the time, and, with so many children to feed and care for, we as parents had to become beyond experts at multi-tasking.

It was lunchtime, and I was preparing lunch for our toddler. From the kitchen, I could see my wife, sitting on the couch, with one baby nestled in her lap, a bottle balanced with a receiving blanket, another over her shoulder being burped with one hand and the third on the couch beside her, a bottle in my wife's other hand. I knew I had to capture that moment. The look on my wife's face also reveals exhaustion, but there is a sense of peace and contentment upon her face, vastly different from the unease on the faces of the couple in the black-and-white photograph.

Are we better parents than that couple? Absolutely not. We are, like them, doing the very best we can for our children with the tools we are given.

I wish I could sit and drink tea with that couple, who would undoubtedly be elderly people by now, if they were still alive. I would love to hear their stories, share tales with them, connect as parents of triplets and, all the while, validate their experiences.

I would have loved to have been able to include this photograph as an illustration in this book. I desperately wanted to include it. However, one can imagine my surprise and shock when I discovered that the original copyright holder of the photo stipulated that, when it was acquired by the particular archives in which it is held, it never be permitted for publication in print. I was unable to acquire the permission to use it. Now, one can speculate as to the reason for this. Was the photographer aware that they were documenting an event that would one day be seen as inappropriate? Were they aware of the implications of what was depicted? Did they know it was wrong, and want to keep it hidden? This is my supposition. We may never know. It does not take much snooping around on the internet to find this image, so, alas, I can do little but suggest that you do so.

It's a tough gig, this parenthood business. It's the toughest gig of them all, and I am happy to play it.

10-42, Return to Base

July 13, 2015
Montreal Lake Cree Nation, Saskatchewan

After two weeks of intense fighting, the rains came and we stood down. Two weeks of battling some of the worst fires in Saskatchewan history.

I had been about sixty feet into the bush, in dirty, soot-covered overalls and fire boots, with fifty pounds of equipment on my back – a ten-pound plastic, hand-operated fire pump and twenty litres of water, which weighed around forty pounds. I was in an area of bush that we had thoroughly soaked down already, but there were hot spots that still required putting out, using a brass nozzle that you slid back and forth like the pump action on a shotgun. I heard the first drops of rain hitting the plastic of my hard hat, then the dull splat as it hit the ashy ground at my feet.

The author lying in the grass after receiving the order to stand down while fighting fires, Montreal Lake Cree Nation, Saskatchewan, July 2015.
© Jan Cej, used with permission.

When the call came over the radio to fall back, I let out a deep breath. I walked out of the bush, put my equipment down, lay down in the grass and closed my eyes, with my hard hat on my chest. It was over.

I didn't know my battalion chief snapped a photo of me lying there. It is a very beautiful photograph.

The 2015 fires that raged across northern Saskatchewan that summer led to the largest evacuation in Saskatchewan's history. According to the Red Cross, thirteen thousand people were evacuated from their homes as around 112 fires burned that summer. Calls were put out for any rural, First Nations or volunteer fire departments willing to spare firefighters and equipment to travel north to fight the blazes.

Even the Canadian Armed Forces were deployed to fight the fires.

The fire department I belonged to was not sent up by the Government of Saskatchewan to fight the fires. We went up ahead of the call. The Montreal Lake Cree Nation are our neighbours, and they were losing structures. The wildland fire crews were not able to deal with structure fires. People were losing their homes. Our command volunteered our crews to help our neighbours in need, and we as firefighters, in turn, volunteered to join the crew going seventy kilometres north to fight the fire.

Driving into the community was like some postapocalyptic scene: smoke and charred trees, zero visibility and manned checkpoints. There were times when the road ahead of us could not be seen through the thick smoke, and we proceeded slowly, like driving through a snowstorm, unable to see past the hood of our truck, the red flash of our lights reflected in the smoke. There was the sound of choppers overhead, like an episode of *M*A*S*H*, and all around us was the emptiness of an evacuated community.

I remember the Chief of Montreal Lake thanking us with tears in his eyes for being there. I am proud to say that after our arrival on the fire line, Montreal Lake did not lose another structure to that fire.

Unless one has been on the front lines, it is hard to describe the heat, the noise, the smells and the emotions of facing a wall of fire that can move faster than you could ever dream of running and is consuming and destroying everything in its path, from the air to the earth itself. The awesome majesty that can be created when the conditions are just perfect. When a fire creates its own weather, it can move itself in astounding ways.

I hadn't set out to be a firefighter. It was not on my list when we were inevitably asked as children in school what we wanted to be when we grew up. The field had never spoken to me, and there had never been anyone in my family or in my circle who had chosen firefighting as a career. I come from a long line of military veterans, and I had even tried, once, to enlist. In 1999, I was a young man on a brief stop in Edmonton, trying to figure out what to do with my life. I saw a recruiting poster for the PPCLI (Princess Patricia's Canadian Light Infantry) at a job fair and decided to enlist.

When I got to the kiosk, the recruiter asked me many questions, one of which was "Can you swim?"

I could not swim then, nor can I swim now. I said, "No, I can't swim."

He said, "If you can't swim, then you can't join."

I was crushed, but accepted it and walked away.

Had I been successful, I would have most likely been shipped over to Afghanistan two years later.

I have always felt terrible about it, and have had a sort of survivor's guilt in the fact that I wasn't able to serve in uniform as so many of our Elders did, as my grandfathers did and as so many able-bodied people my age did. In spite of this, being a firefighter never even entered my mind.

When my wife and I originally bought our house out in the rural area she had grown up in, I had no idea of the role the fire service played out in the country. In fact, prior to my joining the department, I had had only one encounter with firefighters, and that was when I experienced a massive vehicle fire the month before my wife gave birth to our daughter.

In retrospect, I probably should have been more aware of the fire department than I was at the time, as we heated our ramshackle wooden farmhouse back then with wood heat, and when you spend every day and most of the night during a bitterly cold Saskatchewan winter going down into your basement and feeding logs into a fire inside your home, it's probably a good idea to know a bit more about how things work.

Then in the spring of 2009, I was driving home late one afternoon along the long, isolated highway that leads to my house. About a kilometre or two from my yard, I caught a glimpse of something in the tree line that ran alongside the road. I only saw it for less than a moment.

When you drive on rural roads in Saskatchewan at any time, day or night, your eyes are never far from the ditches, as you never know when an unexpected whitetail deer will decide to run out in front of your car. As a result, while I kept my eyes on the road, my peripheral vision scanned the ditches for any sign of movement.

All I saw was a glint of light, no more than a flash, but it was enough for me to take notice and slow down. As I approached where the glint had come from, I could see the smallest wisp of smoke rising from the ground, back farther in the bush, almost unperceivable if you weren't looking at that exact spot. I stopped and looked skyward, and I saw the dangling power lines that drooped like unwound guitar strings from the poles to the ground. I also saw the start of flames in the dried cattails where the line had landed.

I quickly drove home as I did not have a cellphone and dialed 911 to report a downed power line and fire, saying that I would be waiting for help at the scene.

The fire trucks arrived very quickly, and the crews got out to survey the area. The fire chief, a man roughly my age, looked over at the fire and said, "You really saw that from all the way over here?"

I said yes, and then he said, "Have you ever considered joining the fire department?"

In the summer of 2010, I applied to join the Lakeland and District Fire Department in Christopher Lake. This rural fire department is among the largest in Saskatchewan, serving four municipalities in a service area approximately 1,540 square kilometres. I was trained in fire suppression (both structure and wildland), vehicle extraction, first aid, emergency medical response and many other skills required to save lives and property. In 2010, I was certified as a first responder, which trained me to respond to 911 emergency calls, and, in 2012, I became certified, with honours, as an emergency medical dispatcher, which would have allowed me to work as a 911 dispatcher.

During my time with the fire department, I attended numerous fire-related calls, EMS calls, motor vehicle accidents and several fatalities. But I will never forget the first time I fought a structure fire from the interior of the building.

It was in December 2010, just around the holidays. The radio rang, and we were dispatched to a structure fire not far from my house. En route, there were reports that possibly there were people trapped inside.

I was certain that, by the time I arrived on scene, other, more experienced crew members would already have the fire knocked down and the situation handled, and I would be outside spraying water onto the exterior of the structure. This was not the case. I was the second crew member on scene.

As we began to fight the fire externally, the fire chief arrived, surveyed the situation and said that we were moving in for an interior attack through the front door. He looked at me and said, "You're backing me up."

I was a rookie, still only a few months into the role. However, with the possibility of lives at risk, I strapped on a tank of air, and followed the chief inside through the front door.

Now, unlike the movies, an interior attack does not involve barging in and spraying water from the hip like a Tommy gun. Firefighters are trained to crawl into buildings carefully, always maintaining an exit route in case the situation goes sideways.

The fire chief went in first, and I followed, keeping a firm grip on his leg to let him know I was still there.

I could feel the intense heat of the flames through the knee pads of my turnout gear. "That's pretty hot!" I remarked, as we inched forward, dragging our hose with us.

We were about six feet into the structure when the floor began to give way beneath the fire chief. I could see him starting to fall forward, almost in slow motion, as the floor beneath him, burned nearly through, started to buckle, aiming to throw him down into the basement of the burning house.

I reached out, grabbing him, and I pulled him back away from the hole in the floor. After a brief moment, he gave the signal to back out of the building, and we did.

Nothing was said about it until the next training night, when he thanked me in front of the rest of the crew for grabbing him before he went through. I thought nothing more of it, until the night of our annual appreciation dinner, where, in front of the community, I was awarded a pin from the department for saving his life.

The events and sights I experienced and witnessed during my time in uniform will remain with me for the rest of my life. I have seen the destructive power of things far beyond fire. I have seen the result of vehicles slamming into each other at excessively high speeds. I have watched as a plow wind tore through a campground filled with families, throwing twenty-metre-tall spruce trees onto RVs and campers, trapping people inside. I have watched a massive heart attack take the life of a loved one before they even hit the floor, their eyes forever locked forward as we tried our best to save them. We then remained with the body for hours until the coroner arrived. I have watched as every single possession of a family, all of their belongings, their photographs and memories, were destroyed by flames as they lost their home. I have seen the destruction of a drunk driver behind the wheel of a car, and many more memories that I will never be rid of.

My personality started to change. I was starting to get angrier and more sullen. I began to have very little patience. I was snapping at my kids; I was being an asshole to people. I wasn't sleeping, and when I did, I was having horrific nightmares. Once, I was dreaming that a call came in over the radio and while asleep I jumped into my vehicle in the middle of the night and began driving to the fire hall. I woke up while driving, clutching a television remote in my hand like it was my fire radio. I am lucky that I did not kill anyone or myself.

The last call I was on was an EMS call one bitterly cold December night in 2015. I arrived to find an older gentleman, his eyes staring skyward. I knew that he was long gone, but I still went to work, trying my best to bring him back, the other people in the house wailing, begging me to save him. As I began chest compressions, fluid from his mouth flew upward and landed in his eye. The eye never blinked. It seemed like forever before I had someone to relieve me. It was nearly twenty minutes of chest compressions, on my own. The roads were icy and treacherous, so it took some time for other units to arrive. For two solid weeks, I could still feel the strain in my forearms and the pain in my fingers from doing chest compressions, and I could still hear the massively loud siren and computerized voice of the AED, the automated external defibrillator, as it continued to say in a monotone voice, "NO SHOCK ADVISED." I couldn't sleep, I couldn't eat and I was dangerously close to falling off the wagon. It had not been my first fatality on a call, but I knew then that it would be my last. I left the fire service in January 2016 due to the effects of post-traumatic stress disorder and other personal issues.

I always said that "if that radio stays silent, then one of our neighbours is not having the worst day of their life." I think of one man in particular, who has been with his fire department since 1980, who has sadly had to respond to countless EMS calls where friends and neighbours did not make it.

Ask any firefighter, active or otherwise, and they will be the first to tell you that dangerous situations are simply part of the everyday experience of the job. However, there are times when the call of duty goes beyond the normal level of dangerous, especially for those who serve or have served as on-reserve, volunteer or rural firefighters – community members who have chosen to carry a radio and respond to calls. Women and men who, just like professional firefighters, often jump out of bed in the middle of the night or during family dinners, drive along treacherous rural roads in the middle of winter and find themselves fighting to save someone's home and life from fire, performing CPR on people they may have known for their entire lives, cutting patients out of crashed automobiles or rescuing people from other dangerous situations.

Firefighters and first responders are often called heroes. Any firefighter will tell you, however, that they don't see themselves as heroes. Rural, First Nations and volunteer fire departments, though, are full of heroes – they are not professional firefighters, but farmers and mechanics and schoolteachers and retired people and everyday community members, willing to lay their lives on the line to save their neighbours. They answer that radio and get into their vehicle, not knowing if they will be coming home. Many have been left scarred and wounded, physically, mentally and spiritually, by their service. Firefighters and first responders are warriors. They battle an enemy and protect their community, going into dangerous situations while others are running the other way.

When I saved the life of our fire chief, people called me a hero. The public called us heroes in 2015 when we fought those massive fires up north. Again, we weren't heroes – we were just trying to save people's homes and the fact that we did not lose another structure during that fire speaks to the determination and training of our crew.

It was a conversation with my therapist, who also happened to be a volunteer firefighter, that taught me that perception can mean a world of difference.

My career was only six years long, and when I left the fire department my inner bully told me that I quit. I was a quitter. I was weak, and that's why I have PTSD and that's why I quit.

My therapist set me straight. I wasn't lazy, I wasn't shirking my duty. I listened to my body and my body was telling me that it was time to pack it in. I didn't quit. I did my duty, and walked away on my own terms.

He handed me a dictionary and asked me to look up the definition of the word *retired*. I did, and the definition was "withdrawn from one's position or occupation." He then asked me to look up the word *quit*. I did. It said, "to admit defeat, to give up."

He asked me, "Which one would you think best describes the situation?"

I then adjusted the way I looked at the situation, and I regained my dignity. I began to seek out other firefighters online, other people who had experienced similar events, who had a better understanding of what I was going through. I began to build a network of peer support online, sharing my feelings and thoughts with others who had, if not the tools to help me, at least the ability to empathize and understand.

During the course of online PTSD peer support, the subject of medals and decorations came up, and the question was asked about what medals are awarded in Saskatchewan to fire, police and EMS personnel. This subject had me do some research.

In Canada, almost all of the medals awarded specifically to firefighters are for long service. The only two provinces that award medals of bravery to firefighters are Ontario and British Columbia. Saskatchewan offers the Protective Services Medal for those who have put in twenty years or more of service.

I was unaware that the simple question about Saskatchewan medals would change a fundamental way in seeing my role as a firefighter.

I had started out advocating for the government to create a medal specifically to recognize everyday rural and on-reserve volunteer firefighters and first responders – a medal that means more than just "hey, thanks for sticking with it for two or three decades," because many, myself included, don't make it that long.

There is almost nothing out there from either the provincial or federal governments to recognize the everyday efforts of those firefighters who serve their communities; nothing that says, "We thank you for what you are doing and what you have done, and we honour your work." While long service and acts of bravery are important milestones, there should also be recognition for the average firefighter who answers that radio, gets into their vehicle and doesn't know if they will be coming home, or for those whose service has left them scarred and wounded.

My vision for this is something beyond a lapel pin that can be cheaply picked up at a trophy shop or a paper certificate with your name on it. My vision is for something that comes with the pride of being decorated and having your work recognized, of having that medal pinned to your chest, of being honoured by leaders that you served in that capacity. A medal recognizing the work and everyday bravery of volunteer firefighters and first responders would be the only one of its kind in North America. The closest comparison I could find to what I had in mind was the United States' Army Good Conduct Medal, which, according to the United States Army Human Resources Command website, is described as follows: "The Army Good Conduct Medal (AGCM) was established by Executive Order 8809, 28 June 1941 and was amended by Executive Order 9323, 1943 and by Executive Order 10444, 10 April 1953. It is awarded for exemplary behavior, efficiency, and fidelity in active Federal military service. It is awarded on a selective basis to each soldier who distinguishes himself or herself from among his or her fellow Soldiers by their exemplary conduct, efficiency, and fidelity throughout a specified period of continuous enlisted active Federal military service." It is, essentially, a recognition of an American soldier's character, behaviour and actions. It is a goal to strive for, and it is a concept that I wanted to bring to the fire service in Canada.

I began to write letters to various federal, provincial, municipal and fire-related organizations, pushing forward the idea of creating this medal. I was met with almost universal passing of responsibility to various governmental agencies, with the final rejection of "We'll take it into consideration" coming from no less than the office of the Chancellery of Honours in Ottawa, which, as a literary writer of poetry who has received many rejection letters from publishers across Canada, even I admit was pretty cool. I was undeterred, however, and to this day I continue to submit letter after letter to the various branches of government, requesting meaningful recognition for firefighters and first responders.

Now, one might argue that a medal is meaningless, in the grand scheme of things, and that time, money and effort be devoted to the more practical needs of firefighters, such as support for those firefighters and their families suffering from PTSD, care for firefighters battling severe work-related cancers and illnesses, and proper equipment, training and support for underfunded and understaffed departments. This is a fair argument, and one which I have often made myself. The effect that official recognition has upon someone in uniform in this manner, combined with proper mental, professional and emotional support when dealing with matters such as post-traumatic stress and work-related injury I believe can certainly assist in the well-being and care for emergency service personnel. When you know you are appreciated, and you know that you have a strong sense of belonging behind you, it means so much more than when you are left on your own to deal with it, feeling unappreciated and without worth.

This advocacy has been deeply meaningful for me personally on several levels. First and foremost, I hope to advocate for those who won't or can't speak up for themselves. As Indigenous people, we are taught to be humble, and to speak of our glories is considered rude in many Indigenous cultures. Couple this with the added silence of PTSD, and those voices grow quieter still. There is a need for these warriors, which fire and EMS personnel truly are, to be recognized.

This project has also been part of my own personal healing journey. When I left the fire service, I left with an incredible sense of guilt, as well as a lost sense of self-appreciation for the work I had done. The trauma had robbed me of the pride I should have had for myself. As I went through therapy, the therapist suggested that I remove anything firefighter related from my home. I found myself jettisoning anything fire department related. Firefighters are known for their collections of patches, baseball caps, T-shirts and other forms of firefighter memorabilia. I removed all trace of firefighting from my home. Even my decorations – my pin for five years' service and my pin for a life saved – were put away, out of sight, much like my step-grandfather had done with his own medals after returning from the Second World War. I was afraid to show pride in what I had done, because to acknowledge it would have brought back memories that I was not ready to deal with. But by removing all that I had accomplished and the world I had been a part of, I was not allowing myself to address and heal the wounds. The work on this project restored a bit of that self-appreciation. It has been part of my medicine bundle.

I have always wanted to create and foster the culture of first responders as warriors, which we are. When you are in a rural setting, far from the city with the convenience of its hospitals and the swift arrival of an ambulance, you can wait sometimes for an hour for the paramedics to arrive. It can be a terrifying experience. This is the gap filled by the rural and volunteer firefighter and first responder – we are the ones who arrive when you call for help, and it is something that not a lot of people can do. It goes hard against the heart and mind. Sometimes too hard, and you wake up in the night, terrified to close your eyes again. Yet if that radio went off at that moment, you would respond, because someone needed you. Someone was calling for help.

I am quickly approaching a time when I will have been away from the fire department longer than I was on it. What's most heartbreaking is the fact that, since I have left the fire service, not one member of my former department has ever reached out to see how I was doing or to check in. It is as if I am once again a faceless member of society, simply a civilian, out of the circle, out of the "brotherhood." In talking with other former firefighters and first responders, I found that this is a common occurrence, and former emergency service personnel feel forgotten, shunned and abandoned, especially when they are going through some pretty major trauma internally. I cannot explain why this is. I have asked serving firefighters why this happens, only to be met with "No, that doesn't happen," and so on.

I wonder if it is a sign of fear? Is the "brotherhood" afraid that acknowledging that one of their own has PTSD will weaken them? Do they still see it as a form of weakness? Are we still battling this macho, tough guy bullshit? I have no answers.

Through counselling and seeking out help when needed, the effects of my PTSD are becoming more manageable. They will never go away fully, they will always be there, but the nightmares aren't as frequent as they were, and I am slowly able to talk about the calls I attended and how they affected me, though I still feel apprehension in doing so, for there is still that element out there who are quick to dismiss what you have to say, by going, "Really? It was only a few years! You couldn't have been on THAT many calls, it shouldn't have been THAT bad on you." There will always be that sense of one-upmanship and of dismissal, and that, because you "couldn't hack it," you are weak and "should've never been a firefighter in the first place."

I made a choice to live in some of the most visually beautiful locations in the world. In summer and winter, people flock here to take in the stunning majesty and beauty of the northern boreal forest of Saskatchewan. I will continue to live here, in this beautiful land. However, where the tourists can take the scenic drives and routes with impunity, those drives and routes are almost all and forever tainted by the memories of my time in uniform. "There was a snowmobile accident down that trail," "We did CPR on a dead guy for an hour in that cabin," "So-and-so's grandma died there," "We cut a drunk teenager out of a car here," "That family lost everything in a house fire there" and so on.

When I find the dark memories creeping back in, I remind myself that the healthiest thing for me was to walk away, but that doesn't make me weak, and it doesn't take away the honour I earned as a warrior. I just needed to walk away from the fire line, and, at that moment, stand down and wait for the rain to give a helping hand.

The Painting

When I was a young man in my teens and early twenties, I was bad for telling dirty jokes. I used to think they were funny and harmless. No one at the time told me different, and I was often swept up in the momentum of other people telling the same sort of misogynistic and degrading jokes and stories.

It only took one person to say to me, "That was inappropriate," and I stopped, right then and there. It changed my whole outlook on life, and my impact on others, all by one person saying, "You're being inappropriate." The jokes weren't funny then, and they're not funny now.

I am grateful for those who stand up today to share how painful these kinds of things are, and who call it out whenever it happens.

In the tumultuous spring of 2020, a well-known and respected Indigenous artist released a painting wherein a group of Indigenous women were gathered around in what appeared to be a sacred lodge, with Canadian prime minister Justin Trudeau on his hands and knees, his pants down, his buttocks exposed and being spread apart, and a naked woman in a headdress seems to be about to either slap or sodomize him with a red-painted hand. The women around him are laughing and taking joy from all of this. In the background, Justin's deceased father, Pierre Trudeau, is forced to watch helplessly.

I was not prepared for this image in any shape or form. To say that I was appalled would not do it justice. It was painful to see. It was physically painful.

It hurt me on so many levels. As an Indigenous Knowledge Carrier, I saw a sacred lodge being desecrated. As someone who has worked so closely with victims of sexual assault, I saw their experiences trivialized and rape glorified. As a bisexual man myself, I saw the LGBTQ2 community being exploited and used as "punishment." As an artist, I saw the talented hand of someone I had held in high respect and adoration being used to create what was for me, for lack of a better term, exploitative trauma porn.

The term *trauma porn* is often used to refer to instances where individuals will show graphic violence, pain and brutality for little more than shock value, sometimes under the guise of "artistic expression." Most often, trauma porn comes in the form of videos depicting graphic violence, beatings, death and destruction, and they are shared on social media sites. Trauma porn can be as benign as watching hockey fights or mixed martial arts or as brutal as watching graphic scenes of real-life murders. The common theme between it all, of course, is deriving pleasure and entertainment from it. The Germans have a phrase for this: *schadenfreude*, which, roughly translated, means "pleasure derived by someone from another person's misfortune." Whether we like it or not, there is something that draws people to watch another human being suffer.

As I write this, the world was rattled by the interview the Duke and Duchess of Sussex gave to Oprah Winfrey, in which they revealed traumatic experiences with racism, thoughts of suicide and a desire to break free of the constraints and pressures of royal life in order to save their mental health. I had waited for quite some time to weigh in on the current situation regarding the royal family and the interview. I did so in order to ensure that the words I use are honest, truthful and educated.

First and foremost, I would like to say that, yes, I do believe that these two individuals did indeed suffer the experiences and pain they spoke about. The actions of the palace staff and of those individuals who handle the running of the machine are completely reprehensible, and I hope that they both can get the professional and emotional help they require to heal this trauma in their lives.

Do I feel that this should have been addressed? Yes, absolutely. Do I think it should have been done the way that it was, before millions of people? I do not, and I'll tell you why.

I was six months sober when I was first asked to speak in front of an audience about it. Six months, that's it. I stood in front of a room full of strangers and spoke about my trauma and my addictions. I ripped open wounds still seeping, wounds that were not even beginning to heal yet. There was no safety net, nobody there to catch me or debrief me, and I fell off the wagon shortly thereafter. I have watched too many individuals thrust out before audiences too quickly, with only a small time of sobriety under their belts. I have watched them crash and burn in the flames of the spotlight. It takes time to heal, and when you're beginning to overcome trauma and addiction, you need to learn to live this new life and have your feet beneath you for a while before making that leap.

Now, I don't know their story, and what help they have sought since leaving the UK, but even then, it is a traumatic experience to do this for anyone, I don't care who you are, and, in their situation, the attempt to address the abuse they suffered via the very medium that is one of the main abusers is still part of that cycle of abuse. Do not kid yourself, the hosts of that broadcast knew this very well, and under the guise of a nurturing and understanding "friend," did nothing more than join the ranks of those who have taken advantage of and revictimized these two, and walked away from it with a tidy sum of money. These two people have been used and exploited, plain and simple. Once again, trauma porn. Schadenfreude.

Are they completely innocent? Of course not. No one in life is truly innocent, and they are people of extreme privilege and wealth who chose to open themselves up to the court of public opinion in front of millions of people. While it is one thing to look upon this young man as a loving husband and father who has stood up for his young family in the face of racism, we must not forget that this same young man knowingly attended a Halloween costume party at the age of twenty dressed as a Nazi. Many individuals of lesser stature have fallen from grace for much less, and, in the grand scheme of things, he saw very little in terms of consequences for this action. This must be acknowledged, as we are all to be held accountable for our actions. History is often ugly.

But what are the boundaries on consequences? When I first saw the painting I thought specifically of two groups. I thought of the Indigenous women who sat as models for this piece, and I wondered if they were aware of what they were posing for, or had they also been victimized by it?

And though it may not be a popular thought, I thought of Justin Trudeau's children. Politics aside, and regardless of what political machinations have occurred over the years, this is still a human being, a parent of young children who will one day be able to look their father up online and see this image of their father being assaulted while their grandfather, their ancestor, is forced to watch. When one speaks to victims and families of sexual assault, one of the things you often hear is "I wouldn't wish this on anyone." This painting goes against everything that sentiment stands for.

What I was not prepared for, however, was the massive amount of support that the work received, and who defended the piece in the name of artistic expression. The supporters, many of whom were influential individuals in the Canadian artistic scene, defended the work, claiming that it was okay because the painting somehow symbolized retribution of those who have suffered colonization against the Colonizers, represented by Trudeau.

Now, I am not an art critic. I do not possess a degree in fine arts, nor do I consider myself an authority on the subject whatsoever. I did not approach this subject from the point of an armchair academic proclaiming opinions from some self-aggrandizing pedestal of influence. I looked upon this piece as someone who has been victimized and survived traumatic experiences. I am also privy to the experiences of others who have suffered similar traumas in their lives, but who do not have at the moment the personal strength, ability and support to speak for themselves. I am simply another person who chooses to express their emotional state by smearing globs of coloured acrylic around on a piece of canvas. This is the position I speak from.

Fully aware that my arguments could have been tantamount to career suicide, I spent many days following the release of this painting in the usual sort of pitched and heated online battles with those who chose to defend the work on some sort of academic or moral level. I was deeply pleased to see who stepped forward to join the voices speaking for those who could not speak for themselves. I was surprised by a few, for I was sure that their feelings swung the other way on the subject, but nevertheless they added their voices to the fight.

The furor eventually subsided, and the artist provided an apology, to a point, and promised to remove the piece from any online viewing. At the time, I gave them credit for their apology as a good start but felt that more was needed from them to heal the pain caused, and that only time would tell what exactly could be done to heal. As of this writing, all has been silent on the subject.

I still shudder when I think of that painting. I needed to find something good to come out of this whole experience, so I scoured the paragraphs of text fired through the skirmish to see a silver lining. It was by doing this that I came to an important realization.

I have created my own thought-provoking works that have caused reactions in audiences that have been less than positive. I once performed a piece where my simply having an empty coffin onstage as a prop caused audience members to leave. I have often said that we artists, whatever the medium, have one job. We need to cause our audience to feel something, be it positive or negative. We live in a rapidly desensitizing world, and it is our responsibility as creative people to counteract that desensitization with emotional content. By this rationale, one could argue that the artist in question did do this. However, allow me to be clear on this point: wounded people should not have to suffer revictimization as a sacrifice on the altar of artistic expression. Period.

As artists, our job is to make the viewer feel emotion from within, not inflict pain on them. If our work has done this, then we need to take responsibility for our actions and do whatever it takes to heal the pain we have caused. My ability as an artist to self-express does not come at the expense of others' emotions, nor does it provide immunity from consequences. This is the lesson of art as *maskihkiy*, as medicine.

As Indigenous men, a valuable lesson has been lost. When a matriarch or a survivor tells us that we have done something painful, instead of arguing about it, we are supposed to listen, stop what we are doing and make amends. As my wonderful wife and partner always says, "The best apology is changed behaviour." This is *tapahtêyimisowin*, the sacred teaching of humility, of being humble.

Too many artists have forgotten what it means to be humble, and, coming from a colonized view of the alpha male and having to fight for respect from the western world, too many see humility as a sign of weakness. This is a cycle that needs to stop, and we as Indigenous artists need to continue reminding each other to truly listen and be aware. Not out of a sense of "Hey, look at me! I'm woke! Pat me on the head and tell me I'm a good boy!" but because it is the right thing to do.

However, with all this being said, when someone who has been victimized or traumatized finally gains enough courage to make themselves unbelievably vulnerable by sharing what has happened to them and disclosing to others about it, the absolutely worst thing that anyone can do is begin to question, belittle or dismiss their account as false or proclaim that they are lying or exaggerating.

The term for this is *gaslighting*. This is a form of psychological abuse, wherein the abuser will, by denials, accusations, dismissive confrontations and acts of verbal belittling, cause their victim to begin to question whether or not their trauma is real, in an effort to suppress their voice or cause them to change how they remember or recall what happened. This is often to mitigate the actions of the abuser, so that they can go without blame or appear to be innocent of their actions.

The term *gaslight* comes from the 1944 film adaptation of a 1938 play, in which the lead character is slowly manipulated into believing that she is becoming insane, often by the lowering and raising of the gas lighting. For example, the protagonist might say, "The lights are flickering," while the antagonist will dismissively say, "No, they're not," even as they are.

This all boils down to trust. Artists are trusted to create emotional content to send a message, not exploit pain for the sake of exploitation. We as decent human beings should be willing to listen to those who say, "I am hurt. This is painful. This has hurt me."

As a younger man, I cannot say that I gave much thought to those "jokes" I thought were so clever beyond the laughs I presumed they would bring. I wish I had realized that, perhaps, the laughter was just a mask to hide the pain I caused.

There is a line, attributed to the late author Terry Pratchett, that I love. It goes, "Satire is meant to ridicule power. If you are laughing at people who are hurting, it's not satire, it's bullying."

On Writer's Block

When I was a kid, I watched a single episode of a
television series which has stayed with me after all these years.
It was an anthology series based on the works of author Ray
Bradbury, and Bradbury himself appeared in the opening.

I'll set the scene as best as I can: An antique wrought-iron
elevator raises into view, as a very late '70s/early '80s synthe-
sizer plays notes meant to be eerie and mysterious. A figure
emerges, then their silhouette appears behind a frosted glass
door. The door opens with a creaking sound, and the camera
pans down to reveal the figure walking through, without
showing their face.

With the camera following from behind, the grey-haired
figure proceeds to walk though cramped and crowded rooms,
turning on lights as he walks past stacks of books, sheaves of
papers, a white suit jacket on a stand with a straw boater hat,
a cut-out of Mickey Mouse. Photos cover the walls.

He pauses for a moment before entering another room. Every square inch of this room is filled with knick-knacks, tchotchkes and other ephemera, as the voice-over speaks about where he gets his inspirations. He walks around the room, explaining that he draws his inspiration from his collection of stuff, and, as he loads a piece of paper into his typewriter and begins to type, the camera pans to reveal that the collection of objects and junk in this room is extensive.

I was enthralled by this. I grew up poor with few possessions of my own. I recall sitting in an empty apartment as a kid with no furniture, not even a bed, sleeping on a pile of clothing. I remember seeing this television intro and I knowing that I wanted to recreate this world for myself. I wanted to fill an office space with assorted items from which to glean inspiration. Perhaps it was just a lonely child with very little wanting things to own, but I made myself a promise that, one day, I would have that same set-up. I would be a storyteller. Around the same time, in 1992, I was a student of a man named Michael Gatin. It was either grade five or six, at Wild Rose School – a small rural school actually in the middle of NOWHERE. There were kilometres of fields in every possible direction.

Mr. Gatin read to the class the book *Underground to Canada*, by Barbara Smucker. It is a tale of the Underground Railroad, and the journey of slaves in the American South to reach the north, and freedom. To say that Mr. Gatin was a phenomenal storyteller does not do him justice. The way he gave the characters their own unique voices and personalities overrode the monotonous drone that had been my experience of hearing stories read by five years of disinterested teachers.

At that moment, without knowing it, my life was changed in a way that continues to this day.

It's been over twenty years since then. I've been a storyteller now for most of that time, gracing stages across Canada and around the world. I've been blessed to stand in front of classrooms full of children, reading stories, sharing tales and legends, being what we call in Cree *otâcimow* – a storyteller. With every tale told, however, the footprint of a teacher long ago is there, as I try my very best to make the same kind of impression on my students as Mr. Gatin made upon me so very long ago. Thank you, Mr. Gatin, for the gift of the craft.

I'm often told that certain materials like plastic, rubber garden hose or garbage, when thrown into a fire, will burn special colours, like blue and purple and green. I myself have never seen this. My eyes apparently do not possess the ability to process that particular spectrum. Even during my time as a firefighter, when I witnessed many spectacular blazes, like the bright white sparks when magnesium ignites in a car fire, the flames always remained the same yellowy-orange colour for me.

Now, I'm not colour-blind by any means. I'd be a very different type of painter if I were, believe me. The artist in me would, however, love to be able to see these blue and green and purple flames that seem to mesmerize those who take joy and comfort from staring deep into the flames.

Fire has always been a muse for me. Many of the poems I have written were inspired by the flicker of a fire. Indeed, much of what you are holding in your hands at this moment was inspired by a small campfire somewhere across northern Saskatchewan, either in memory or in practice. It is a bit of a ritual for me, to be honest. As summer ends and autumn arrives, I like to take all these little jottings, verses, musings and scribbles I have written, either on scraps of paper or as long-winded social media posts, and transcribe them by hand into small, black, hardcover notebooks. Then, when everything is compiled, I commit them to a manuscript. Everything I write has been written at least three times, at least once by hand, and I will often take those first scribbles and jot notes and commit them to the flames, completing the circle, as it were.

I remember the day that I stopped writing poetry.

I was working on a manuscript. It was the first time in over twenty years that a publisher had shown real interest in my work. They were talking contracts, royalties, book tours, book awards and all the other wonderfully excitable events that come with a book deal. It looked like the start of a new chance as a poet; another start, two decades after I had my first taste of it, my first glimpse into what being a published author was like.

I was on my coffee break at work when I read the email.

The publisher had backed out of the deal. They were only interested in the manuscript if I could successfully translate it into Cree. I had tried, using what little conversational Cree I still had, along with an online Cree dictionary, but I couldn't do it. I told the publisher this, and they walked away from the book.

I tried so very hard not to burst into tears in front of my colleagues, but it was no use. I barely made it to the men's room before I was wracked with heaving sobs. I later told my colleagues that I had the stomach flu and ran like that to throw up.

The tears first came as a sense of failure. The loss of my language scuttling my second chance; colonialization once again rearing its ugly head to hold back an Indigenous person from achieving anything.

It wasn't until later that night that it hit me. They hadn't taken any real interest in my words. They weren't interested in what I had to say as an artist or a poet. They only wanted a book they could publish in Cree. I could have written the shittiest poetry book in the world, and they would have published it, had it been translated into Cree.

I thought back over the past twenty years, over the nearly two hundred rejection letters I had received from publishers. I thought back on how I had committed my deepest thoughts and feelings to paper, and how I had beaten them and mangled them and dishonoured them in order to fit into submission guidelines. I thought of the dozens of anthologies my peers had created and published over the years, how I discovered them on bookstore shelves and how no one had ever even extended an offer to me to submit a piece. I thought of all the emails and messages I had sent to people in the business – publishers and literary agents – and how those messages went without reply. I thought of those peers who went from reading their scribbled words at open mic gigs to publishing deals and literary awards in less than a year. I thought about it all, and it hurt.

It still hurts, truth be told.

The desire to write poetry seemed to dissipate. I felt the words leave me, the words I had held onto so tightly for so long. I knew that I had to let them go. The creative fire needed to go elsewhere, into other projects. The poet in me was gone. At that moment, I didn't know if he would ever be back, and I was at peace with it.

The poet returned, however, and I welcomed him with open arms.

It is tragically fitting, as it were, that I write this at a time where large swaths of the world are on fire. The year began with Australia on fire, and now, upon the cusp of the autumn of a tragic year, there are uncontrolled fires scorching large portions of Turtle Island. These fires, though, do not inspire anything other than grief, so it is also fitting that, given the world at this exact moment, I'm suffering from an odd form of writer's block.

You see, I'm writing a novel where my characters are going to restaurants, staying in hotels, shopping in stores and flying in airplanes, and this is normal routine in their world which I have created.

It's a world that, at the moment, no longer exists for us in real life, and the world I created in my novel has become historical fiction, a time before this deadly disease.

I'm still finding it difficult to write for that world now. I remain petrified of COVID-19, in spite of my double vaccination, as we live in a world where petty, heartless and selfish people refuse to wear masks or social distance. I don't want those heartless and selfish people in my own life, let alone the fictional world I created. I don't want the pandemic in my life or in my writing, yet it is there.

I stare at the last paragraph I wrote before the pandemic. The protagonist sits in a hotel room. He has just gotten off a plane and is considering where he will visit first. There's no concern for the virus, and he is living his life blissfully carefree. That world is somewhat gone forever, and I just can't get back into that frame of mind. I'm sure other writers went through the same thing.

I was once asked, "What is one of your biggest fears in life?" It didn't take me very long to answer. My biggest fear in life would be to go through what happened to Jonathan Larson.

For those who don't know, Jonathan Larson was the writer and composer of the massive Broadway phenomenon that was *Rent*. What few people know, however, is that Jonathan Larson struggled for over a decade to have his work noticed, let alone published, performed and appreciated, and this was in New York City, with connections to people like Stephen Sondheim. He received the odd small commission and gig here and there, some small notions of appreciation from some institutions along the way, but nothing in the way of actual, tangible, meaningful recognition that would consti-tute his creative output as being a "career." Instead, he waited tables and lived in poverty in NYC, writing at night in a small, unheated apartment. He wrote of his life and experiences, as well as the lives of those living in New York City in the chaotic 1980s...and no one was listening. He went unpublished, his work went unperformed and he found himself having to schlep around open mic nights and small gatherings just to be heard. Finally, a small theatre workshop agreed to perform *Rent*. Tragically, on January 25, 1996, the night before the first preview and dress rehearsal, Jonathan Larson died from an aortic dissection. He was thirty-five years old.

In his all-too-brief life, Jonathan Larson did not get to reap the benefits from his work. He never got a chance to

Jonathan Larson, the writer and creator of the Broadway play *Rent*.
© Rich Lee, used with permission.

see the amazing success of *Rent*. His Pulitzer Prize and his Tony Award were awarded posthumously. The financial security that *Rent* would have provided, and the opportunities a successful Broadway show would have given could not be used by him. Most of all, however, he never had a chance to see the millions of people who saw his words and heard his music performed. He never had the chance to see the impact his years of sacrifice would have on so many facets of the world: the theatre world, the LGBTQ2 community, those living with HIV and AIDS, and so many others. Jonathan Larson died alone on the floor of his kitchen on a cold January morning, knowing that only a handful of people had ever heard what he had to say, and fewer still really even cared, at the age of thirty-five.

My story paralleled Jonathan Larson's life in so many ways. I also know the sting of rejection from a community that is so close but seems to be slamming the door on you repeatedly. I know what it's like to play to half-empty rooms, and to set up readings and performances where not one person shows up. I am honoured and blessed to be friends with some of the biggest names in both the Canadian literary and Indigenous literary community, yet my writings continued to go unread and unpublished. I've watched as my peers have skyrocketed to success, while my twenty years of hard work remained at a standstill, and the rejection letters piled up. I've written truthfully from the heart, and had it rejected. I've butchered and mangled my words to meet the demands of publishers and editors, and had it rejected. I've been both the iconoclast and the ass-kisser, toed the line and went against the grain, and still rejected. It hurt, and it is enough to make a person want to give up on themselves and their dreams.

My art sat in my studio unseen and not exhibited outside my community. My books sat unpublished, and my self-published work unsold. Artists create work for people to appreciate, and when no one sees your work or appreciates it, try as you might, you do want to quit and say, "Why do I bother?"

But no matter what, I never forgot where I came from. I was born into a life of obstacles, and I've been overcoming them my whole life.

It's obvious, of course, since you're reading this, that I started writing again. The muse was just too strong for me to fight.

It was upon the shores of Waskesiu Lake, in Prince Albert National Park, where I once again picked up the pen and began to write. Prince Albert National Park lies roughly ninety kilometres or so north of the city of Prince Albert. Established in 1927, the park covers nearly four thousand square kilometres and is nestled in the boreal forest of Saskatchewan.

Although I grew up within an hour or so of the park, I had never visited it as a child, at least, not to my knowledge. It was a place I had heard talked about often, but, growing up in the 'hood, it was out of our realm. It wasn't until I had met my wife and moved north out of the city that I ventured into it. Crossing the park boundary for the first time, I felt the unexpected shiver of connection, like meeting a long-lost friend. As I hiked the trails and walked along the shores of the massive lake, I found myself connecting with the earth in a much more meaningful way than I ever had before. I found inspiration in the landscape surrounding me, and I found the words flowing once again from a place inside which had grown so cold. Tom Thomson, the famed Canadian landscape painter of the early twentieth century and progenitor of the Group of Seven, developed a similar relationship with the lands of Algonquin Provincial Park, and drew inspiration from the things within it to create his masterworks. Likewise, I drew from Prince Albert National Park the inspiration to create both visual and literary works again, and it was this creative medicine that went into my 2020 book, *Childhood Thoughts and Water*, as well as my 2021 book, *Kitotam*. It is part of many Indigenous cultures to go out upon the land and seek answers to questions, seek peace from chaos, seek healing from pain and seek wisdom from the earth. I had not realized that I was seeking a "happy place," a part of the world where I could go and recharge my mental, spiritual, emotional and physical batteries, and I saw for the first time how much of my work was being created from a position of those various batteries being consistently drained. When the Muse and I met once again, in the shade of majestic spruce and poplar trees in northern Saskatchewan, the work produced began to reflect that, and works like the novel have been put to the side for the time being, so that I can devote my time to keeping up with the Muse.

While I have never fulfilled my childhood dream of filling a room full of crap in order to draw inspiration from it – though not from lack of trying, I assure you – I would hope that, in this great global village that we were promised at the dawn of the Internet Age, there would be something inspirational out there in the various rooms that surround us. Well, there is lots out there to inspire, but I really don't write horror stories.

And the single episode of the Ray Bradbury series I mentioned? Ironically, it was about a man who built his own coffin, and whose tale turns rather dark, fittingly.

The Kitchen

One night in 2019, I was picking up my volleyball-playing daughter from the first school where I had ever worked and I had to stop and pay my respects to the school's kitchen area.

In the spring of 2011, I'd lost my dream job. I had spent the better part of a decade working with "at-risk" youth on the front lines as an outreach worker in the downtown core of the city. I loved that job, not only because I was good at it, but because I felt that I was making a real difference in the lives of those I had worked with. They had seen me come up from those same streets, overcome the same obstacles, fight the same demons and succeed.

But it all came crashing down that spring. Decisions and choices were being made around me that I was not, nor would I ever be, okay with. I was being asked to go along with these decisions, which were counterintuitive to everything I had been trained to do. Because I stood by my principles, I watched as my dream died. I was thirty years old. I had a young family to provide for, and here I was, starting over at the bottom. I found a job making snacks in a building where once I was brought in as a consultant, a man with a life-threatening food allergy working in a kitchen. My sobriety teetered on a razor's edge. I pressed on though, because I knew that if I wanted to be able to keep looking at myself in the mirror each morning, I needed to be true to myself.

I had no skill with food and I undertook the position with great worry. I worked as hard as I could, terrified of losing the job. It was a bleak time for me, and my daily commute to and from work was filled with tears. I am barred from kitchen work to this day as any cooking or food preparation now fills me with dread.

Still, I did my very best in this little kitchen. I spent many anxious moments there, not knowing if I was going to make it, but knowing that I would never give up. This was my first step back, my foot in the door.

As I stared at that door in 2019, I began to take stock, as it were, of this life of mine.

By the age of nine, I had spent five years growing up in a residential school.

By sixteen, I was living independently and beginning my path to sobriety.

By eighteen, I began my journey as a professional writer and artist.

By nineteen, I went to the University of Cambridge on scholarship AND "claimed" England for the First Peoples of the Americas.

By twenty, I danced powwow in Australia.

By twenty-two, I had spoken, presented and performed before over twenty thousand people across three countries and two continents.

By twenty-three, I had written a successful book of Indigenous poetry.

By twenty-five, I was on a nationwide book tour, sharing the stage with the likes of Margaret Atwood.

By thirty, I was in uniform as a firefighter and first responder, and was decorated for heroism.

By thirty-seven, I celebrated twenty years clean and sober.

By thirty-eight, I was elected to both the provincial and national levels of CUPE (the Canadian Union of Public Employees), one of the largest labour unions in the country.

Along the way, I became a husband, a father and a Traditional Knowledge Carrier. I have devoted my entire adult life to working with youth, and I have been an activist for Indigenous, LGBTQ2 and refugee rights, the environment, anti-racism, those dealing with addictions and poverty, and first responders dealing with PTSD.

I soon realized something. You can wait all you want for someone to recognize your achievements in life, nominate you for awards and medals and pat you on the back. But if you don't take stock yourself, and proclaim how far you've come, and recognize your own victories, all that you have accomplished so far may be forgotten, even by you.

There is no shame in owning your victories. This was a difficult lesson for me, as it was counter to the Indigenous traditional belief of humility. Being humble is one of the core teachings of the tipi, and boasting of your achievements goes against that.

Because of this I try to keep a balance between the victories I have won and remembering the costs of those lessons. There was a lesson I learned many years ago which has stuck with me.

Take a fresh piece of paper and crumple it into a ball. Then flatten it out as best as you can. Apologize to the paper, once or repeatedly, but say that you are sorry and that you regret crumpling the paper. Proclaim to the world that you have apologized to the paper, that your actions are not who you really are, that you respect all paper and that you never meant to wrinkle the paper. You could devote the rest of your life to learning about paper, and use your voice or your position to decry the injustice faced by paper, become an ally or a champion of paper, donate money or volunteer, and hope "that we can all move on from this…" Tell people that you crumpled the paper a long time ago, and that you've changed your ways, and that you hope people see you as the person you are now, not the person you were when you crumpled the paper.

In spite of all you have done to "better yourself" and "atone for your mistakes," I ask you this:

Are the wrinkles and creases gone from the piece of paper?

Have your apologies and good deeds removed the damage you caused?

Has the paper been restored to the way it was before you crumpled it?

You may have learned from your actions, and you may never do it again, but the damage you caused never goes away, and nothing you do will ever erase your actions. Your apologies mean little to nothing to truly fix what you have done.

The lesson? Perhaps you should never have crumpled the paper in the first place.

In many Indigenous cultures, we speak of forgiveness. That being said, there are things like physical and sexual abuse that are beyond forgivable, and nothing you do with your life will erase the damage you have done.

I remember being curled up on the floor in a filthy public bathroom in a gas station, my face against the cold porcelain bowl, sticky with other people's urine. I was not yet seventeen years old, but I was trying so hard to numb and drown the pain wracking me physically, mentally and emotionally, successfully hiding it all from my family to the point that, to this day, many deny that it ever happened.

That night, however, I finally knew I had to make a choice, and I made it.

I made a choice to walk away from the damage I was doing to my body. I didn't quit right then and there, and the struggle to stay sober in those first few years was immense, but I made a choice. I slipped so many times, but I kept getting up every time I slipped, until my footing was finally firm under me. Nearly twenty years since my last major slip.

I've since seen the world and have told my story in front of thousands of people on three continents, have had my paintings upon the walls of galleries and my words in print around the globe. But these are not my greatest achievements. My

The author as a very young man. Author's photo.

greatest achievement is that my children have never seen me drunk, never seen me passed out on the floor, ripping chunks of flesh with my fingernails to free my arms of the bugs I swore were under my skin. I have tried my very best not to crumple their papers.

My body is broken and my health is ruined, but I am still here. I get sick at the drop of a hat, but I am still here. I've watched as my friends died around me, knowing the pain they were going through, and I'm still here to tell their stories.

I've crumpled my own paper too many times.

Over twenty years ago, I made a choice to try my best to stop crumpling my paper. Every morning that I wake up, I still make that choice. Every morning. Because, no matter what, I can still feel that cold, piss-smelling porcelain bowl on my cheek, and I never want to go back to it.

216

Recently, I turned forty years old. I will be completely honest – I did not expect to be here this long. For much of my life, I was convinced that I would not live past the age of twenty-seven. I had from childhood a premonition that I would not make it to twenty-eight years of age, long before I knew of the "27 Club" and its famous members. Ironically, Kurt Cobain and I share the same birthday, and this was the first year since his death that I have not played a song or paid my respects to him.

Prior to my thirtieth birthday I suffered a minor heart attack, the result of excess weight, substance abuse in my teenage years and stress. It was certainly a wake-up call, and I did not take it lightly. I began to see any time after that as borrowed time, and I have tried my very best to fill up as much time as I can with activities and projects, leaving very little for idle moments or "downtime." I also became focused on getting back to a slimmer, physically stronger body.

The weeks leading up to my fortieth birthday had been different for me. After a year spent in full-on creative mode, creating a staggering amount of paintings, videos and poetry, as well as trying to complete a major manuscript, I hit a creative wall around the end of January. It was a complete stop, and the output ceased abruptly. An injury had left me barely able to walk, and I found myself doing what I dread the most – absolutely nothing.

Was this the universe sending me another sign, a reminder of the checkmate I dodged ten years prior? I do not know. What I do know is this – what you are reading is the most substantial thing I have written in weeks. I cannot count the times in the past few weeks I have opened my laptop, opened a Word document, stared at it silently, then closed it.

Will the same thing happen tomorrow? Maybe, but I do know that it did not happen tonight, and that is a good thing.

I often look back at photos of that time in my life, photos of a much younger me, a long time ago. I look, and I ask myself, "Do I miss this guy?"

Well…

I miss his youth. I miss his long dark hair and his thirty-four-inch waist. I miss the black silk dress shirts that hung off his slender frame and the biker boots. I don't miss the life he was living, though, and I don't miss the missing pieces of the puzzle. I don't miss the things he did to deal with the pain.

But I do miss the way he looked.

Okimâw

I remember a long time ago, at a traditional powwow somewhere in Saskatchewan, when the Elders warned the powwow committee about the new metal centre pole in the arbour, which is the dancing area of the powwow grounds. The traditional way is and was for a wooden centre pole in the arbour. The committee wouldn't listen, however, saying, "No, no, it'll be alright." That day, the first day of the powwow, just as we had completed the first Grand Entry, a big gust of wind came up and ripped that metal centre pole out of the ground, along with the parachute that had been used as an awning over the arbour. The rest of the powwow was cancelled. The leaders were not listened to in the beginning, but they were listened to afterwards.

The Nêhiyawak word *okimâw* means "leader, chief, a person in high position." However, when phrased another way, it can be interpreted to refer to a "big shot, someone who thinks they're better than you."

I come from a long line of chiefs, and I remember one of my *nicâpânak*, great-aunts, saying, "The way you used to tell which house on the reserve belonged to the Chief was that it was the emptiest. Everything he had belonged to the people, and you could walk in and take what you needed, and that was his way."

In many Indigenous communities of the twenty-first century, the stereotype of a Chief is one of corruption, excess, nepotism and genuflection to Ottawa. It is, unfortunately, a stereotype based in reality and a look into our history shows this. I remember the words of the late Allan Longjohn, Elder from Sturgeon Lake First Nation, as he spoke to a nearly empty room in 2007 – a room supposed to be filled with over seventy Chiefs from Saskatchewan reserves. "When that person in your reserve puts an X in your square, he expects you to be here in the meeting, and to go home and bring what you have learned from the meeting itself and the people you have met here."

We must also remember that the position of "Chief," in regards to the role after the signing of treaty, was laid out and described by Alexander Morris, Lieutenant Governor of Manitoba and the North-West Territories, this way: "The Chiefs and head men are not to be lightly put aside. When a treaty is made, they become servants of the Queen; they are to try and keep order amongst their people." Earlier on the page, he states, "Chiefs ought to be respected, they ought to be looked up to by their people; they ought to have good Councillors; the Chiefs and Councillors should consult for the good of their people."

My great-great-great-grandfather Chief Mistawasis, first signatory of Treaty Six, said, "Our way of living is gone, there are no more buffalo, we have to find a new way to feed our people." My great-uncle Joseph Dreaver, chief of the Mistawasis band and one of the founding senators of the Federation of Saskatchewan Indian Nations (now the Federation of Sovereign Indigenous Nations), said, "Give us responsibility, and we shall be found worthy of it."

The role of "Chief" as we know it today is a western concept crowbarred and sledgehammered into a thirteen-thousand-year-old way of life.

The role as I see it now is to find that balance between the juxtaposition of both ways – the way of the twenty-first-century politician and the leadership required of traditional Indigenous culture. The balance should be buttressed on both sides by the desire to provide a healthy existence for the People in the long term, not in short spurts. Long term – as Long as the Sun Shines and the Waters Flow. Our Chiefs must not forget this.

We will continue to look to our leaders and representatives for guidance and we hope that they will make the best decisions for all of us. However, our leaders are human, and they are easily susceptible to the human vices of avarice, power and corruption. These are as old as humans themselves. I am not one to gaze at our pre-contact ancestors through rose-coloured glasses and say that they were without malice or greed. However, I do feel that those leaders carried themselves with the honest hope that what they were doing was best for the People as a whole. They had to, because that type of leadership is necessary to survival in the harsh physical climate we have lived in for thousands of years.

Carrying It Forward

The ideas and practices of a democratically elected Chief and Council system are, by their nature, colonial constructs, forced upon us by virtue of the Indian Act and by examples set for quite some time through our various governance systems. It is, in all honesty, a foreign construct crowbarred into Indigenous existence to the point where we see it now as it sits: precarious, constantly shifting, untrusted by many.

Will we ever return to a place before contact? No, we won't, no more than we returned to a world before September 11, 2001, and no more than we will to a time before COVID-19. My hope for the future is that we return to a remembrance of a time when the community ensured that no one went without, no one suffered unduly. Once upon a time, it was starvation and disease that threatened the people. Today, there is so much more that needs to be done.

When we talk about reconciliation, we must remember that we as Indigenous people are NOT the ones who should be doing the reconciling. We are the affected who are to be reconciled with. When doing so, that means everyone. If your idea of reconciliation doesn't include street people, those in the sex trade, the homeless, the intoxicated, the kids in gangs, the incarcerated, the Listerine drinkers and those shooting meth, then it's not really reconciliation. They are victims of colonization, too, and they too must be cared for.

Those in any position of power, perceived or otherwise, must ensure that all people are cared and provided for. If you cannot do this, then, frankly, get the hell out of the way and let someone else do it.

In Conclusion

There you have it, a glimpse into the thoughts and feelings of someone who has achieved a miniscule amount of notoriety and attention because of a mediocre ability to put words and phrases into a particular order, the ability to smear globs of pigmented acrylic across a stretched canvas to form somewhat recognizable images, the biological connection to a group of men who helped shape the Canadian Indigenous landscape decades before his birth and an event that took place over twenty years ago and six thousand kilometres away, which was sparsely attended and poorly covered in the media, all of which would have been forgotten and overlooked had he not continued to bring it up over and over again for years at every opportunity.

When I was a younger man, I had an inflated sense of self-importance, a feeling that I was going to do big things and be more successful than I ended up being. My head was filled with grandiose fantasies in the hopes that such successes would fill the many painful holes and gaps within myself, so that, as an adult, I would no longer be the over-looked and forgotten face I was in childhood, noticed only by the bullies and by those who exploit the vulnerable. The fact that I didn't succeed to the level to which I had hoped was a painfully hard lesson to learn, but it was a lesson for which I will be forever grateful. It taught me humility, what it means to be truly humble, and what it means to work for the betterment of the People as a whole.

It also taught me a terrifying and sobering lesson about the dangers of instilling into young people the idea that success and financial gain and fame is the be-all and end-all, that this is the goal for which you should strive at all times, otherwise your life has no worth or value, and you have wasted it. The fall from such a lofty perch is a devastating one, for not only does it hurt the bird, but also those whom the bird hits and crashes into on the way down.

The biggest takeaway from it all, for me, is how hard I fought – and, in many ways, continue to fight – to be recognized and accepted within the Indigenous community, and particularly, for some reason, by complete strangers on social media who I am never likely to meet in person. I believe it still stems from that need to feel accepted and acknowledged, which came from a childhood disconnected from my community. That connection was broken by the residential schools long before I was born and long before I grew up in one. That emptiness and the lack of feeling accepted and connected is one which I feel will never completely go away. I remember the first time that I ever heard about the Looking

Glass Self put forth by Charles Cooley in 1902, which states that some individuals base their self-worth on what they believe that other people think about them. It was as if I had been hit by a ton of bricks. My entire self-worth was based, and to some extent still is based, on what I assumed others thought about me, and if I wasn't being acknowledged, then I must have been worthless. This insight enabled me to take the first steps to reconcile within myself my struggles to be whole and my often-quixotic attempts at recognition. Make no mistake, those thoughts are still there. If I walk into a room and two people are whispering to each other, I still wonder, "Are they talking about me?" As I write this, I find myself acknowledging the mental yo-yo of it all: I want people talking about me, yet, if they are talking about me, is it in a negative context?

As I move forward in life, continuing to unpack the multitude of well-hidden cases and boxes deep inside the rooms of my memory palace, I am fully aware of the tightrope balance required to ensure that what I say and do is not for me and me alone, but for all of the individuals with whom I have contact daily, either in-person or virtually, in one of the various capacities in which I serve, be it as an artist, a storyteller, someone's connection to their culture or their past, an educator or father and husband. While this may sound like a common, everyday experience for the majority of some, remember that, with me and many others like me, it is filtered through many layers of poor self-esteem, anxiety, fear and long-guarded emotional instability. I must take care that my words harm no one, including myself. I mentioned earlier in this book how an Elder would place a knife before them and offer their listeners the chance to use it upon them if they did not agree with the Elder's words. Now, imagine hundreds of proverbial knives a day, in various situations, placed before dozens of listeners and dozens of interactions, while, at the same time, finding my own mind placing its own knives in front of my self-esteem and self-worth. It can be a bit tricky.

I remember as a child always being asked in school that most ubiquitous of questions, "What do you want to be when you grow up?" Given the circumstances of my life as a child, it was impossible for me to answer truthfully. In my career working with youth, I've heard children answer this question with the usual choices of firefighter, police officer, doctor, hockey player, singer and so on. I've heard extremely wealthy children at the age of ten parrot what must be their parents' words and say that they want to be the CEOs of corporations or own their own luxury resorts. On the other side of that coin, I will never forget the nine-year-old child early on in my career who straight-up told me that they wanted to be a drug dealer when they grew up. When I asked them why, they said, "So I can get money, then go to jail." This was the life and the example set for them, and it broke my heart so badly that, as I'm writing this, I am crying. If I can help it, I no longer ask young people what they want to be when they grow up.

I don't remember what answers I gave as a child when I was asked that question. I must have said something, if only to get the teacher off my back. I honestly have no memory of any answers. I didn't have the luxury of thinking that far ahead.

In Conclusion

As I move forward, farther out from my youth and the emotional chaos of my first twenty years, I know that I do value the slower pace of life I currently live. I am in a ramshackle farmhouse in the middle of nowhere, on the edge of the northern boreal forest, living with my amazing family with simple pleasures. I watch as many historical documentaries as I can; read as many cheesy British cozy mysteries as I can get my hands on; collect as many dusty and well-played LPs and 45 rpm singles as I can; raise my chickens and my ducks; create as much art, poetry and literature as my periodic artist's/writer's block will let me, all while continuing to be an advocate and warrior for those who need it, and at the same time continuing the unending work of learning my culture and language in order to pass it on to the next generation. I know that saying my life is a work in progress is such a cliché, but, for the most part, it is. It is a continual process of healing, redeeming, teaching and learning. I am the perpetual student, and what I learn, I want to share. Perhaps that's what I have always wanted to be, *kiskinwahamâkêw*, a teacher.

My existence is not that far off from the life my grandfather chose to live in his small cabin in La Ronge. It is a simple existence, which, after the life I've led, is fine by me. If I wasn't there to live it, I wouldn't believe it myself. I'm glad, however, that I kept the receipts.

Epilogue

It's 3:00 a.m., the last day of January 2022. I haven't had a proper sleep for days, as anxiety, trepidation and all-out fear have gripped my mind and spirit.

For days, the images and Facebook posts of the so-called "Freedom Convoy" have filled the screen of my phone. Photos of screaming, maskless, right-wing zealots and eighteen-wheeler trucks have bombarded me. The streets of Ottawa are filled with throngs of people spewing horrible, vitriolic, anti-vaxxer, anti-Trudeau rhetoric. The protestors have defiled the monument to Terry Fox, the Canadian icon who tried to run across Canada with one prosthetic leg to raise money and awareness for cancer research. They hung a sign around his neck, tied a flag around his throat and slapped a "trucker" hat on his head.

Ambulances and paramedics have been pelted with rocks. The staff and patrons of a soup kitchen for the homeless were threatened with violence for not providing food to the protestors. Racial and homophobic slurs have been hurled at passersby. Sitting Members of Parliament have been threatened with violence, their home addresses being sought out by the mob. The sitting prime minister and his family had to be removed from Ottawa to a secure location for fear of their safety.

They pissed on both the National War Memorial and the National Aboriginal Veterans Memorial.

They danced upon the Tomb of the Unknown Soldier.

There are swastikas and Confederate flags flying on Parliament Hill.

Think about that for a second: there are white supremacist flags flying on Parliament Hill in Ottawa, Ontario, in 2022.

I think back to the Black Lives Matter demonstrations of only a few years ago. I think back to the Idle No More marches, the blockades of the Wet'suwet'en in their own territories and of Oka. I remember the throngs of heavily armed law enforcement officers deployed against peaceful demonstrators, the threat and use of military action against them. I remember Conservative politicians calling for the physical removal by force of people standing up for the right to be treated with basic human decency and for the right not to be killed or go missing. They called for laws to ban groups from gathering in this way.

Those same Conservative politicians welcomed this mob with open arms. The Ottawa police have essentially refused to get involved. They say that they are afraid to engage, for fear of violence. Some have posed for selfies with the protestors.

I've watched as people I have known and loved for years, people who I assumed were good, decent individuals who knew better, have thrown their support behind the mob. They are, at best, willfully ignoring the racism and hatred, making statements to the effect of "they don't speak for me," and "there's always going to be some bad apples," or, at worst, not only condoning the racism, but supporting it.

The past few days have taken a severe toll on my mental health, perhaps more so than at any other point of the pandemic. This has severely messed me up inside, just as the events of January 6, 2021, in the US did, when Trump supporters stormed their Capitol. The hatred, the racism, the huge masses of negativity that these people are pushing forward; the hypocrisy of politicians and law enforcement; the double standards of how extremely violent, right-wing, almost exclusively white mobs are treated as opposed to peaceful, organized and lawful mass gatherings by groups of colour; the comments sections of news stories; the laughter emojis on stories decrying the actions; and hundreds of other little microaggressions have had a cumulative effect on my body and mind.

Throughout this book, I have talked well and often about my grandfathers, the roles they played both in my life and on the world's stage. As veterans of the Second World War, they witnessed and faced first-hand the horrors of a world when right-wing fascism is given the opportunity. It pains me to say it, but I am glad that they aren't here to witness this. I'm glad that they went to the Spirit World in a time when they knew that they had defeated Nazism on its own territory. I'm grateful that they did not have to see the enemy's flag flying on Parliament Hill.

I often say, "What a much better world it would be without Conservative politics." I know that this is a massive oversimplification. However, the amount of horror in this world caused by puritanical zealots of all stripes accounts for much of human history, from the Crusades to today. It may be painting many people with a broad brush, but, unless you are actively speaking out against violence, racism and hatred, your silence is complicity. There is no longer room for the devil's advocate or seeing both sides on these issues. To quote Elie Wiesel, noted writer and Holocaust survivor, "Neutrality helps the oppressor, never the victim. Silence encourages the tormentor, never the tormented," and "The opposite of love is not hate, its indifference."

In spite of all of this, in fact, because of all of this, I still ask the same question to both lower and upper case C conservatives:

Why?

Why do you hate so much? Why does the thought of caring for one another, loving one another, making sacrifices for one another make you so bloody angry? Why does asking for basic human rights such as clean drinking water, a healthier planet and protection from life-threatening diseases anger you so much? Why the greed? Why the violence? Why do you believe that your existence and convenience is more important than others?

I cannot fathom that mindset. I cannot comprehend that level of angry hate. How can a human function with that much anger and hatred in their bodies?

If you are among those who go out of your way to say, "But I'm not like that. They don't speak for me," then I also ask you why.

Why do you remain silent? Why do you not speak out?

It's hard to see a light at the end of the tunnel, when it feels like every minor victory is merely a sandbag holding back the flood waters.

Meanwhile, people are dying, while selfish bigots scream about their "freedom." Their freedom to hate, their freedom to live without consequences for their actions, their freedom to destroy the world around them for their own personal gratification.

I mourn the dead. I mourn those who we have lost to COVID-19, but I also mourn the living dead, as it were. I mourn the death of the people I thought I knew. I mourn the people who, though still walking the earth, are now dead to me. I mourn the loss of the friends I thought I had.

The coyotes are howling in the fields outside my window. The weather is turning, and there will be massive amounts of snow blown across the empty fields of the Saskatchewan prairie. I refill my cold cup of tea and listen to their cries while trying not to doomscroll on my phone until the sun comes up. Their howls are pure and kinder on the ears.

John Brady McDonald is a Nêhiyawak-Métis writer, artist, historian, musician, playwright, actor and activist born and raised in Prince Albert, Saskatchewan. He is from the Muskeg Lake Cree Nation and the Mistawasis Nêhiyawak. He is the author of several books, and his written works have been published and presented around the globe. He is also an acclaimed public speaker, who has presented in venues across the globe, such as the Ânskohk Aboriginal Literature Festival, the Black Hills Seminars on Reclaiming Youth, the Appalachian Mountain Seminars, the Edmonton and Fort McMurray Literary Festival, the Eden Mills Writers' Festival and the Ottawa International Writers Festival. A noted polymath, John lives in Northern Saskatchewan.